The Savvy Guide to Kick-Starting your Small Business
*- Advice to small business owners on **survival** and **growth***

To the four ladies in my life...

Ruth, Amy, Jenny and Joan

The SAVVY GUIDE *to* KICK-STARTING *your* SMALL BUSINESS

Advice to small business owners *on* survival *and* growth

Ian Marshall

The Savvy Guide to Kick-Starting your Small Business

*- Advice to small business owners on **survival** and **growth***

First published in 2015 by
Panoma Press Ltd
48 St Vincent Drive, St Albans, Herts, AL1 5SJ UK

info@panomapress.com
www.panomapress.com

Cover design by Michael Inns
Artwork by Karen Gladwell

ISBN 978-1-909623-85-9

Contents

Acknowledgments

HAVING SPENT more than 40 years working in a broad variety of businesses, I've met and worked with some very smart people, many of whom have kindly taken time out to share with me the wisdom they've gleaned from their own business experiences – for this I am most grateful.

My wife, Ruth, a GP since 1982, as a partner in a large medical practice has faced many challenges typically experienced by any small business. Over the years she and I have, over a glass of wine, discussed our work challenges and bounced ideas off each other; this, in so many ways, has inspired new ideas for me and provided greater clarity.

Wendy Crayden, my business partner, has also been most supportive and much of what we have learned together, in running our business, has provided material for this book.

Over the years I've read and researched much literature provided by those who have enjoyed the ups and suffered the downs of running a business, and feel immensely grateful to them for sharing their experiences for the benefit of those of us who will inevitably have to tread the same path.

I am immensely indebted to the many people who provided much help and support in the creation of this book. Their comments and suggestions have contributed hugely to the finished article. I'd therefore like to extend a big thank you to…

Mark Amory, Monica Berrangé, Mark & Sara Bishop, Leon Gomez, Sam Crawford, Andrew Macmillan, Lorna Pissarro, Ian Saunders and David Wiltshire.

Last, but certainly not least, I must pay tribute to the clients I've worked with over the years since I started my accountancy practice. There are far too many of them to name but I can tell you that, collectively, they have taught me far more than I ever taught them. Above all they have shown me that we can all do better if only we're prepared to step out of our comfort zone and try something different.

CHAPTER ONE

Setting the scene

"SAVVY", FROM the French verb *savoir*, to know, implies a little more than just knowledge. Rather, it suggests a streetwise ability to apply information not necessarily available to everyone – you could call it having an inside track.

The savvy small business owner – and I assure you there are plenty such people out there – has successfully worked out how to get their business from where it once was to where they needed it to be. However they, and most successful business people like them, will not have got there overnight: they will have zigzagged along a route of trial and error – a great deal of trial and a host of errors!

This learning process is important and necessary for the development of any business owner who seeks a stronger business. But, how much time, effort and anguish could you save if you had your very own personal guide to help you avoid so many of the pitfalls that can beset you on the challenging path that lies ahead? The pages that follow are aimed directly at giving you that inside track.

Where are you now?

Perhaps you're about to embark upon your very first enterprise and you're concerned to ensure that you build your new business on a firm footing for achieving lasting business success. On the other hand you might be a battle-hardened business owner in a rut and deeply worried that you could be working the same long hours for a pittance 15 years from now. Or maybe you've just survived the ravages of a recent economic downturn – by the skin of your teeth – and fervently wish for a business that is not quite so vulnerable to what's going on "out there".

Whatever stage you are at with your business, in the pages that follow you will be introduced to a systematic approach that will give you crystal clear clarity about how to strengthen your business, increase your income and how to spend less time doing it.

I'll show you how to deal confidently with problems and go for goals with laser-like focus and I'll explain how and why your own continued personal development will support the growth of your business.

Finding those golden threads

What are the key ingredients of business success? This is a question that has, as long as I can recall, been a source of true fascination for me. Analysing, researching and learning from other people's experiences as well from my own, I have to say, has brought many rewards and no small number of surprises.

As I began my journey of learning and development and read of the experiences of those who had gone before, one very crucial question occurred to me at an early stage: *What do consistently successful businesses do consistently well?* In other words, what common themes exist that are applied by those businesses that achieve better than average results year in, year out?

What I found is that certain underlying foundational principles apply, across the board, irrespective of the type, size or nature of the business or indeed what industry a business may operate in, that can be universally applied. True, in each business they may be applied in marginally different ways and in different measure but there can be no doubt that there are common threads we can all apply that can make a huge, positive difference to any business.

A bit like a honey bee

I've been most fortunate in having had the opportunity to work with such a large number of business owners in a broad range of industries.

I must confess that, acting as a consultant, I have learnt at least as much from my clients as they have learnt from me. A truly effective consultant, I would suggest, is one who can learn from clients' mistakes, challenges and wisdom, then apply that ever-growing bank of knowledge and experience for the benefit of everyone... a bit like the way a honey bee operates I suppose.

Moreover, I've been able to apply what I've learnt over the years, to my own business – so I can tell you from first hand that the systems and techniques to which you are about to be introduced are truly tried and tested... and they work!

A very practical guide for you...

Don't worry; to achieve the success you seek you don't need to be a natural leader, a marketing guru or a financial wiz. Nor indeed do you need to have any academic qualifications. When it comes to running a business successfully there's really no substitute for learning from experience: your own and from those who have already trodden the path that you are about to take.

Drawing from the Macrays *BusinessForward* consultancy programme, in the pages that follow I'll be introducing you to the practical steps you need to follow to achieve success for your business. Primarily I'll be focusing on four key challenges common to most small business owners. These are:

1. *How to increase your business and personal income…*
2. *How to run a successful business and still have a life…*
3. *How to make your business better able to survive the tough times… and…*
4. *How to build real value in your business so that, should you decide to sell it, you can maximise the price you get.*

That said, as you'll see, the principles to which you're about to be introduced can be applied to any business goals you seek.

What's more, you're *not* about to be bombarded with clever theories or smart sounding buzzwords: *this is a practical guide* for dealing directly with the key challenges you face as a small business owner.

Most barriers to achieving what you really want stem largely from a fundamental lack of understanding about what really makes a business tick. So I'm going to home right in on the key issues, strip away the mystique and debunk many of misconceptions that surround the whole subject of *business success*.

How to get the best out of this book

In the following pages I'll be covering a broad range of business topics. You will no doubt have strengths in some areas and weaknesses in others – so if you wish to dip in and out or focus on areas where you feel you're weakest then please do so: each chapter and topic covered stands on its own and will help you greatly whether or not you read preceding or following topics.

However I should tell you that, with this book, the whole is very much greater than the sum of the parts and you will gain far superior overall benefits from working through the chapters in the order presented.

Note I used the verb "working", not "reading". *I advise you treat this book as stimulus for action.* Do not make the fatal mistake of promising yourself you'll come back to a particular section some time later – start to set out your new action plans and formulate your ideas right now!

Right from the start, keep asking yourself this key question: *If I were to take action on this right now, what would be my first step?* Then write it down and make a commitment to act on it. You can never make something happen next week or tomorrow, you can only take action right now, in this moment – so start with your action plans. If something occurs to you in the moment, capture it immediately; that thought or idea may never return!

Overview

CHAPTER 2 – *It's all about you* is aimed at giving you, the business owner, a new perspective: one that helps you find an approach that supports you on every level to achieve your aims, whatever they may be. We start by freeing up your time and focusing your efforts so that you're only ever doing that which you need to do in order to achieve what you want.

CHAPTER 3 – *Taking hold* explains why you need to take a leading role for your business and how to go about it. If things are to change, someone has to make it happen!

CHAPTER 4 – *What your customers want* focuses on the most crucially important activity for your business: *serving the needs of your customers* – for if you're not achieving this, you don't have a business!

CHAPTER 5 – *Your powerful proposition* homes right in on the very core of your overall marketing approach: your powerful marketing proposition. This shows you how to match your products and services with what your customers really want and get your message across.

CHAPTER 6 – *Take control of your profits and* **CHAPTER 7** – *Cash when you need it* will introduce you to some very smart moves you'll need to make if you want to increase your profits. It also takes you through a step-by-step process of how to seize control of the cash available to you.

CHAPTER 8 – *Getting the funds you need* looks at getting clarity about the why and how of borrowing money and some insights into other forms of finance. Making the right moves here can save you huge amounts of cash and a lot of heartache.

CHAPTER 9 – *Getting better all the time* shows you why written systems and procedures are indispensable for your business and how you can easily introduce them without spending *any* time writing them out yourself!

CHAPTER 10 – *It's a people business* looks at the significance of people power plus the *how* and *why* of building strong relationships for the future prosperity of your business.

CHAPTER 11 – *When the going gets tough* lays out how to take control when your business runs into difficulties and how to avoid the traps that so many small business owners fall into in the midst of a crisis.

CHAPTER 12 – *Pulling it all together* rounds it all up and draws together all those Golden Threads that permeate any savvy business.

OK, so let's get started ...

LEGAL NOTICE

This book is intended to be a guide on how to strengthen and grow your business. Any concepts, ideas or theories explored herein must be tailored to your own business needs and are not intended to provide a specific outcome. No warranties whether implied or expressed are given whatsoever in that regard. You are at all times encouraged to take appropriate legal and tax advice to ensure that the procedures you apply to your own business are suitable and appropriate to achieve the outcomes you seek.

The author, the publisher and its agents accept no responsibility whatsoever for any failures to achieve any outcome, or any liability whatsoever arising from your following any act or direction contained in this book without first taking appropriate professional advice. Nothing in this paragraph seeks to exclude liability for fraud, death or personal injury, or for anything else for which it may be unlawful for us to do.

CHAPTER TWO

It's all about you

WHERE YOUR business is right now is the result of the sum total of all the choices you've made, for good or bad. Use the wrong approach and your business takes a backward step, a smart move or two and things start to improve. Strengthening your business is about making smarter choices, so this chapter is aimed at showing you what smarter choices look like and getting you to focus your efforts on what's really important to you.

Let's begin by giving you some much needed breathing space so you can start giving your business some serious love and attention...

More time for you

If you can't organise yourself, how can you possibly hope to organise your business? If you're struggling to find the time to develop and grow you need to make some changes, not only to the way you do things but, more fundamentally, to *the very way you think about the way you do things.*

In this section I'm going to introduce you to a different perspective: a way of looking at how you do the things you do and how you can do them with much greater focus and in less time.

We'll kick off by grabbing some quick wins so you can free up some of your time right now. Then we'll move on to look at how you can create, for yourself, a powerful sense of focus and structure in everything you do – so you're giving your attention to *only* that which is *important to you* and doing it in the right order. OK, let's look a little closer at what it's all about...

Giving you breathing space

The ability to organise yourself effectively, and indeed all your resources, is perhaps *the* most fundamental business skill of all. Get this right and *every* aspect of your business will benefit, on every level. Believe me; it's worth really putting some serious effort into getting this right because it will pay you dividends many times over!

This is not just about time management, it's much more foundational than that – if I had to put a label on it I'd call it "self leadership". Getting your act together on this can have tangible benefits that will permeate so many aspects of your business and indeed your life; the true payback is incalculable!

The double bonus of the Savvy Business Process

Just think: if you could develop a real skill that not only allows you to take control of your business but also frees up your time so you don't have to sacrifice everything else in your life to achieve it, wouldn't that be worth working for?

OK, now I've whetted your appetite, let's take a look at some of the key tools and perspectives that will help you really take control of your workloads and your life.

Smarter not harder

Just so you know, right from the off, I'm not going to be asking you to work harder, more intensely or longer hours. Rather, I'm going to show you how to tighten up your focus so that more of what you do is geared precisely to that which you are seeking to achieve; no more, no less.

Let's be clear here, I want you to focus on doing what you need to do in order to achieve your goals – everything else is just a distraction – and believe me you can waste an obscene amount of your time on distractions. Come on, be honest with yourself, you know you're guilty of this, right? So a key time saver for you here is to develop a habit of making sure you're not getting side-tracked – but how do you do this?

Avoiding the time wasters

Here are some especially powerful techniques for saving time and getting you focused...

Do you really need to do it?

You can start your own personal development by creating a really potent new work habit: from now on, before you begin *any* new task, just for a moment, stand back and consider whether this task really needs to be done at all. Consider carefully what would happen if you simply didn't do it?

Of course, in the vast majority of cases you *do* need to carry out the tasks that are part of your daily and weekly routines but you should find, particularly if you've never carried out this exercise before, that you can cut out upwards of 10% of your current workload almost immediately! Think about it: if you could cut just 5% of your ongoing workload, for the rest of your working life, what difference would that make to you?

Stay relevant

Seek out tasks that have suffered inertia – these are possibly jobs you were asked to carry out, on a regular basis, quite some time ago that, when the request was first made, was considered necessary. However, circumstances may have changed, and it could be that no one bothered to tell you they're not needed anymore.

If you don't know for a fact that the task you're carrying out still has value to you and is consistent with what you're trying to achieve then check it out, challenge those who are asking you to carry out that task – if you can get it off your plate the potential for time savings, particularly in the long run, can be huge.

Reports for no reason

On agreeing to provide a loan to a client of ours, the bank required regular, quarterly management figures. This is not unusual but it can be onerous for a very small business with limited resources.

Three years later, when the loan had been paid off, the borrower had forgotten that those management figures had been linked to this loan and therefore, quite unnecessarily, continued to spend valuable time and effort producing a detailed report that nobody even read – what a waste!

Are you sure you're not making a mistake of the same nature right now? *Never, never, never* just assume all tasks that land on your plate absolutely have to be done – life doesn't work like that. There may be numerous examples of tasks, jobs and responsibilities which are, in reality, nothing more than a complete waste of your time!

Say "yes" for the right reasons

Have there been times in your life when someone has asked you to do something and although you really didn't want to get involved, you did it because you just didn't feel comfortable saying "no"? We've all been there, right? So you agree to help, through gritted teeth and then wonder why you'd been too weak to just refuse.

Some of us have a pathological need to ingratiate ourselves with other people and, conversely, there are those who recognise this in others and mercilessly have them running around after them.

Do you, for example, waste time by agreeing to provide "added extras" that customers request but are unwilling to pay for? If you do this habitually then you're potentially wasting a huge amount of your non-replaceable time.

You need to be polite but firm with those who would take advantage of you in these situations, while themselves giving nothing in return. *Your time really is just as precious as your money* and you wouldn't give that away in great chunks, would you?

The *Savvy Business Owner* knows that there are many people they have to deal with who have their own agenda, who will waste their time trying to get them to donate their energies or money, buy products and services or help with surveys, etc – and they won't get drawn in.

Be on your guard and tough with yourself. You need to be clear on what you want to do and to achieve and stay focused on that. If what you're being asked to do by others is consistent with your values and your goals then fine but if it isn't then say "no" – say it politely, firmly and immediately.

Avoid the scenic route

To my shame, I must confess that when I started working in my first accounting role, I quickly became an expert in the art of finding the most difficult and circuitous way to do any task. Consequently I wasted stacks of time "going round the houses".

Fortunately, my boss, who was exceptionally well organised, took me to one side and gave me guidance. Once the problem was identified for me, tackling it was quite easy. And here's a golden rule I learnt at an early stage: just keep asking yourself: *is there a quicker way to get the same result?*

You'll achieve the best results here if you can develop a mindset where you are constantly seeking out a better way of doing everything you do – this is a habit that *all* successful business owners have.

Remember, the ideal solution to any problem is something you seek, something you constantly aim for – it's not something you can expect to find immediately! The act of seeking it though, is crucially important here as it ensures a continuous process of development and growth. Just think – where could you be in five years' time if at that point you could look back and say honestly that during that period your business had constantly been getting better?

Small is beautiful

Don't blinker your thinking by looking only for the big win – if you can shave a little bit of time and effort off just 50% of the things you need to do, you'll be amazed at the time you can save!

A key point to remember here is that real business success is not, as the media might sometimes suggest, achieved solely by major earth shaking events but rather it is by a continuous process of small improvements and adjustments. *Do not* underestimate the significance of the cumulative effect of a large number of small wins!

Make time to save time

Occasionally I've been informed by clients that they're so busy they don't even have the time to seek out ways of saving time! I'd suggest that it's not time that's lacking here but rather their genuine commitment to business and personal growth. If you are truly committed to making this process work for you then *you will make the time* and remember, we're not asking for any major commitment initially. Give me just a couple of hours of your time each week, at the outset, and I'll show how you can expand that time more and more so that, eventually, you can spend as much or as little of your time as you wish, on developing your business... yes, really!

There's always a better way

I like to challenge clients on their assumptions about the best approach to what they do – and one common response I get is: "Well, that's the way we've always done it". Sorry guys, but that just isn't good enough – there's no such thing as a perfect approach and if you're looking you'll always find scope for some improvement. Just because you can't think of one right now, it does not automatically mean there isn't one.

If you're training someone else to carry out a particular task, ask them to challenge you on the way it's done; can they think of a better way? Coming at it from a new angle could provide a revolutionary new way forward. Be open to new ideas from a fresh mind and be aware of how your own familiarity with a particular task can blind you to a new approach.

Mañana mentality

When you're busy and under pressure it's so tempting to tell yourself that you just need to get that task done and that you'll take steps to change the way you do it later. This is a dangerous way of thinking that easily develops into a habit of putting off any kind of development to some unspecified point in the future – it's a kind of *mañana* (tomorrow) mentality but, regrettably, when you get into this groove *tomorrow* never comes.

If you come across a quicker or better way, when you're working on a task, it's worth taking the time out now to set up that new approach – if you leave it until later you are greatly diminishing the chances that you will do it at all. Don't forget also that the sooner you start to employ your new way the sooner you benefit from it.

Short-term thinking

In my experience, there's a real conflict here in the minds of many people. It's as though we have an inherent need to get the job in hand done as quickly as possible, in this moment, while ignoring the benefits of taking slightly longer to reorganise the task so that it can be done a little more quickly, or in a more effective way in the future.

Let's say a particular task you perform on a weekly basis takes you an hour to complete. Would you spend a one-off, couple of hours now to save yourself (say) 15 minutes each week? The temptation, of course, is to put up with that extra 15 minutes because, quite frankly, you just haven't got the time right now.

If you apply the same logic each week, you'll never make the change. If you really think about it, though, putting that two hours' development work in now will mean that within eight weeks you'll have gained all that time back and after a year the full benefit in time will be more than six times the initial cost! What's more, if this task is likely to be ongoing for more than one year, the overall time savings start to dwarf the initial time expended.

If you start to put that little bit of extra time in now over (say) the next three months – how many tasks can you shave some time off? Cumulatively, how much time can this process start to save you each week? Be careful here – do not dismiss this approach out of hand as being unlikely to have any significant positive effect upon your time – cumulatively this can make a *truly massive* difference!

Hold that thought!

OK, I accept that due to circumstances outside your control, there will be occasions when, as you're carrying out a task, a better approach will occur to you but you really can't take the time out to change the system right now. Just don't allow that great idea to disappear into the ether!

New ideas, methods and approaches for saving time will occur to you, fleetingly, as you are carrying out your day-to-day tasks – such thoughts are sudden, random and momentary. As quickly as they occur to you, they fade from your memory and become lost forever. To allow this to happen is a shameful waste of the power of valuable innovations that can drop into your thoughts from your subconscious.

So steal yourself from whatever it is you're doing at the time (I mean it, be tough with yourself on this!), break off, just for a couple of minutes, and make a note of that thought or idea, so *the very next time* you review this task you can take the time to make the necessary changes and reap the benefits.

Write down how you do it

Have you ever sat down at your desk to start a particular task you've carried out before, but can't remember how you did it? We've all experienced this kind of mental block, right? What comes next is called "reinventing the wheel" and it's a criminal waste of your time!

If you write just the briefest of notes concerning the steps in any routine procedure you'll speed up the process – no doubt about it.

Another advantage of doing this is that having a written procedure makes it much easier for you to train someone else and therefore to delegate.

Later we'll be looking in more detail at systematising many of the key areas of your business, but for now, just start freeing up some of your time by making some basic notes on how you do what you do – if you're having to relearn a task every time you carry it out you're definitely working harder, not smarter.

Avoid: "It's quicker to do it myself"

There are times, as I'm sure you know, when you could delegate a particular routine task to someone else but, right now, you're in a hurry or, perhaps, you just feel you want to get it done as quickly as possible – so you do it yourself.

Of course if you've never shown anyone else how to carry out the task in hand then, naturally, it's going to be quicker *on this one occasion* if you do it yourself. However, if you truly wish to develop and grow your business then you're going to need to start learning about, and getting involved in, leadership and management activities – and that means you have to start letting go of the more mundane day-to-day stuff.

Sure, it's going to take more of your time, on this occasion, but henceforth you can delegate the task and save yourself comparatively *far more time*. We're not talking peanuts here; apply this approach in the way you work and it will make a colossal difference.

Have you have heard the term "gearing"? In this context *gearing* means carrying out a task yourself that will have the effect of saving you many hours work, in the future, by having that work carried out by someone else. So if you're prepared to spend one hour that, over the next year, will save you 100 hours – your one hour was time spent on a *highly geared* activity – believe me the savvy business owner will aim to devote *most* of their time and effort on highly geared activities!

This really is a no-brainer, but when under pressure your instincts will mislead you into believing you're better off just getting it done – so you do the task yourself. If you catch yourself doing this – stop immediately! As owner, and therefore leader of your business, you need let go of tasks that absolutely don't exclusively need your attention.

TIME OUT!

Your main concern right now may be with saving money. On the other hand you may feel that never having enough hours in the day is your key challenge. Of course, for many of us it's both.

If you're confronted with these concerns, but feel you really could do with an extra pair of hands, then you're probably agonising over whether it's better to struggle with the workload and save money or spend the money and save some of your valuable time. I'd like to suggest you may be able to actually improve your income by spending money on getting some help!

Here's a simple rule of thumb that turns that argument on its head. If you can save yourself time which you can then apply to earning more money than you'd pay someone to help you with that routine work, then it's a clear-cut decision – no doubt about it – you should hire yourself that extra pair of hands... and do it now!

What is "Real Work"?

I was once involved in an extremely fruitful strategy meeting in which a team of us was able to make some serious progress on a problem that had been a source of some concern to many key managers within the company.

However, there were a number of team members present who never really got involved in the process; a point that concerned and disappointed the rest of us. Why was it that some key managers never quite showed much enthusiasm for the development process? As the meeting closed, one such individual, as he was leaving the room, smiled and tellingly remarked that he was pleased the meeting was over so that he could now get on with some "real work".

This was the first time I'd come across the difficulty some people have in viewing the planning process as a productive activity. But, of course, I soon came to realise that it's a common feeling and because of it, people don't recognise they are achieving anything or making progress unless they are dealing with the more tangible day-to-day routines where progress is more apparent and measurable.

If you're going to operate more effectively then you have to take on board that planning and organising your time and resources *is* real work and that it is crucially important to the future of your business. What's more, planning work of this type is sometimes urgently required though it hardly ever appears so – don't be fooled!

Pssst… You can't do it all yourself… pass it on…

It's no big secret: the most obvious way to save yourself copious amounts of time and effort is, of course, to delegate stuff to other people. For many small business owners this is far easier said than done. But why?

Delegation is not something that comes easily to everyone. Some people just prefer to do it rather than supervise it. Others feel "If you want it done right it's easier to do it yourself" or "It's quicker to do it myself than show someone else"... and the list goes on. You only have to look at any well-known business with a strong reputation to see that the process of delegation can be made to work effectively... if there's a will.

Of course, there's no point in delegating a task to someone who's not suited to the work involved or who hasn't been trained or hasn't been told what's expected of them. A process of delegation is *a must for a growing business* and you can make it work for yours with the right approach.

If you don't have any employees right now, then of course it's not so easy to delegate routine tasks. Note, I said "not so easy", I didn't say impossible. One obvious option is to *outsource* some of your routine tasks to other businesses who specialise in such services. For instance, you should find it quite easy to make contact with small businesses in your locality that provide typing and secretarial services, thus taking some of the strain of admin off your hands. Alternatively, a local bookkeeper could relieve you of much of the work entailed in the very time-consuming task of maintaining your accounts.

Look for ways to delegate routine tasks that you've been holding on to – this also can provide quick and massive wins for you!

Real benefits of letting go

Because a restaurateur client of ours was determined to a keep a close eye on the finances of his business, he set about doing all the bookkeeping himself. However, his was a very busy restaurant, which not only absorbed virtually all his time in the day-to-day running; it also generated a huge volume of bookkeeping entries.

Gradually, the quality of the records declined to a point where they were no longer a reliable source of information and eventually he took our advice and employed a part-time bookkeeper.

The effect that this had on his business was both immediate and dramatic – suddenly he had more time to take control of the business and he was able to determine, for the first time, not only how much cash he had available but also how profitable his restaurant was.

A bit of nip and tuck

OK, let's start to get some perspective here – the steps I'm outlining in this section seem like a whole lot of work, right? Of course they do – they are a whole lot of work – which of course brings us back to our underlying problem; where do you get the time?

To begin with you only need to allocate the smallest amount of time from your busy weekly schedule. I'd suggest no more than two hours – if you can spare more than this, great! Surely you can find two hours in your week to dedicate to moving your business forward!

Now, if you concentrate your efforts for just two hours each week on nothing other than freeing up your time – what's going happen? OK, I give in – if you can't guess I'll spill the beans: you're going to create yourself *more time*! Capisce?

So what do you do with that time? Yep, you've got it, you carry on working on this section and save yourself even more time... and so on... go on, indulge yourself and really milk this one!

OK, no rocket science involved here, I'm sure you will agree – but if you put some serious effort into this and you appropriately apply that extra time to saving yourself progressively more time – you'll soon be able to build some real momentum in the development of your business.

Would you like me to give you a target here? OK, why not aim to take the amount of time you can spare up to half a day a week and let's say you're going to try and achieve this in six months. Whatever you do, don't go too far too early with this – never take your eye off the day-to-day stuff, after all in the short-term you've still got to serve your customers and pay the bills, right?

This section will only take you so far – the real time-saving stuff comes a little later – but can you now see how you can start to move things forward? It's not about working harder, but rather a little bit of "nip and tuck" and working smarter!

Getting laser-like focus

One body, one brain…

All right, let's tell it as it is. You have only one body, one brain and one set of limbs and if you want to do anything well then you really can only do one thing at a time. I mean it, don't allow yourself to get confused with all this talk of *multi-tasking* – people who apparently do this are not doing several things at the same time, but rather, they are frequently switching tasks. This is more easily done where the nature of the work being carried out is repetitive and easy to do on autopilot. When you're dealing with day-to-day, minute-by-minute decisions and choices that are crucial to your business, your thoughts need to have laser-like focus and not be continually dodging about!

So we've established here that to do anything well you need to focus on that one thing and give it your full attention. Now if you really think about it, *this is quite liberating*! I say this because although you can't effectively do more than one thing at once you *can* control what order you do things in. Given that this is the case you can and should only concentrate your efforts at the start of every month, every week and, indeed each day, on getting your priorities right.

Only so many hours in a day

If you were to make a list of everything you'd like to do in your life you might be surprised what a long list it is. I once carried out this exercise myself and came to the very definite conclusion I couldn't do it all – even if I lived for another 100 years!

The same principle applies to a single day: there's rarely enough time to do everything you want and that's without the unforeseen problems and the numerous interruptions, not to mention the occasional chronic miscalculation of how long a particular task should take – let's face it, it's too easy to be over optimistic.

It doesn't matter how well you plan your day, for one reason or another, the chances are there'll be items on your to-do list that simply won't get done. The brutal fact to take on board here is that there just isn't enough time to do everything you want to do and you need to accept this. *Don't fight it, relax into it*, and act accordingly.

He who works harder

He who works harder will try (and invariably fail) to deal with this problem by working late, through lunch breaks or through whole weekends! This is fine occasionally – when there's a one-off urgent deadline to meet – but to try and do this on an ongoing basis is a bad idea; it's not sustainable and, what's more, it's doomed to failure!

Anyone who works this way doesn't need to prioritise – to him it doesn't matter in what order he tackles the tasks that face him – he's planning to complete them all anyway. This is in spite of the fact that, in the past, he has persistently failed to achieve 100% of everything he sets out to do. Nonetheless he remains optimistic that today will be different... but it never is. High- and low-priority tasks are mixed in together, more or less at random – so, at the end of each day some relatively minor tasks that could have waited have been completed, while some high-priority jobs have been left unattended. Not very smart, eh?

He who works *Smarter*

The *savvy* operator accepts that he can't do it all: he knows he's working with limited resources (resources are *always* limited!). So his first priority is to... well... prioritise!

He'll determine what's most important for his business, and he'll work through his list of tasks *in that order*.

This is what *you* need to do – determine the order of importance of each of your tasks and deal with them, one at a time in that order. It's called planning out your time and unless you have good reason to change your priorities, once you've set them, you *must* stick to them.

TIME OUT!

A key point – and you need to listen up here because this really is a key point! – is that, *no matter what else happens* in your busy day, with this approach *only the least important tasks don't get done.* I'd like you to think very carefully about the implications of that!

Relax and accept

Working smarter is accepting that in any planning period – whether it is your working day, week, month or beyond – you're *not* going to be able to do everything you want to.

Accept that while there are many things that are important to you in your business, and in your life, some issues are more important than others. Focus first on those strategies, plans and tasks which contribute to your most cherished goals and then, if you have the time and energy to achieve some of your lesser goals, great – but if not, accept that this is a price you have to pay for focusing on what means the most to you. If you weren't already convinced of the importance and significance of prioritising surely you are now!

Important or urgent?

It's well documented that we humans frequently err when it comes to differentiating between important and urgent. Any particular task sitting in your in-tray is, to some extent important and urgent or important but not urgent. If you have items in your in-tray that you classify as not important, *what on earth are they doing there?* Before you carry out any task, that task needs to pass the importance test. If it has no importance but is urgent, I suggest you bin it… urgently!

OK, so what's important?

I'm not going to fudge this one, I could just tell you if it's important do it, if it's not important don't – unfortunately, however, life's never quite that cut-and-dried. It's not as simple as one or the other – there are many shades and levels of importance and what criteria should you use anyway to determine what's important to you?

Threats and opportunities will present themselves in so many varied ways and if you're prepared for those challenges you will inevitably learn from experience how to improve the quality of your judgment calls. You will (and should) develop your own unique style – there's no real substitute for experience. However, you can benefit from the experience of those who have gone before and learn from their mistakes. Here's a powerful framework based upon that experience:

   ✓ **Importance,** *for you, is determined by what your goals and targets are and what you wish to achieve in your business and indeed your life. Don't worry, I'm not going to leave you hanging on this one. As you'll see in Chapter 3, I address the setting of goals, etc and I'll be looking at how you apply this to the process of managing your workload.*

   ✓ **It's not just about your medium- and long-term goals though** *– you have to balance all your priorities and that means everything relating to short-term survival too. You may not feel* *that filing your tax returns, for example, particularly helps you with your long-term objectives but if you don't file them you'll get fined and could even go to prison – so dealing with your taxes does have a place in your list of priorities.*

✓ **Don't fall for the comfort zone trap.** *Doing a particular task first just because it's easy or you enjoy doing it, is a bad idea. Remember, once you've determined your priorities, that's what they are; they don't change just because you feel more comfortable dealing with the familiar.*

✓ **Just because it's urgent it doesn't mean it's automatically important** *– don't confuse the two. If, for instance, you're getting pestered by a sales person who's breathing down your neck for a meeting, agreeing to make an appointment may seem like something you need to do urgently, but the key question here is: does this meeting fit with your objectives, or just theirs?*

✓ **Don't let your emotions get the better of you.** *If it doesn't fit the above criteria, ask yourself why you feel you nonetheless need to carry out that task at all. Do you need to do it or is it that you just want to do it? Be honest with yourself – if you're not, you really can waste a huge amount of your energies.*

✓ **If something is both very important and very urgent** *then you need to deal with this first and above all. A word of warning, however; if your working days are a constant procession of very urgent, very important tasks, take it as a sure sign there's something fundamentally flawed about the way you're working!*

Your five-point work plan

Much has been written on how to improve personal efficiency. Of course, becoming efficient is really important but your first aim, in all your endeavours, should be to seek to be effective.

In this context, effectiveness is about making sure you *should* be doing the task in hand – it doesn't matter how efficient you are at carrying out any particular task, if you don't need to be doing it at all then you're wasting your time, even if you are doing it efficiently.

To become more effective as a leader and a manager you need to ask yourself the following questions whenever you're faced with a new task...

1. **Does this task need to be done at all?** *If "Yes" then go to question 2. If "No" then make sure you know where the bin is!*

2. **If it does need to be done, do I need to do it?** *If you can delegate it or outsource it then do so; remember there's only so much you can do, so, wherever possible, delegate those tasks others can help you with.*

3. **If it needs to be done and I need to do it, when do I need to do it?** *If you've got more urgent priorities now then don't blindly bump the task in hand up the order of play – schedule your work so you have plenty of time to get it done, for when it needs to be done.*

   If you're doing this task repeatedly, keep reviewing your options on delegating it. When it comes to admin work, you are not endowed with any special powers; most tasks of this nature can be delegated. Why haven't you delegated it before? Were they good reasons? If they were, do they still apply?

4. **When I carry out this task, what's the most efficient way of doing it?** *You need to constantly seek out better, quicker ways of working, and when you find a better way, implement it even if takes a little extra work on the front end.*

5. **Estimate how long the task will take** *and then add on 20% for good measure, then allocate the time between now and the point where it needs to be done – so you're doing the work without the pressure of being on the last-minute hop!*

Getting it in perspective

Watching a huge aircraft in flight is always an awesome sight for me. I mean, how does that massive 300-ton hunk of metal stay up there in the sky? If you think about it, there are a huge number of factors which all need to work together simultaneously and failure of any one of them could cause that jet to fall to earth. It's impossible to argue that having enough fuel is more important than having a pilot or a rudder, many critical factors need to be in place... or it all fails!

The same principle applies for your business. You can be really good at marketing but if you can't deliver a half reasonable service your business will fail quickly. You can be good at marketing and service delivery but if you can't manage your cash-flow, you'll crash and burn. You can be really strong on all of these but if you're unable to turn a profit you're about to experience a nosedive. So here's an important message to take on board right now...

> **There's no one single thing you can do to make a successful business...**
>
> **... you need to get a combination of factors right, at the same time.**

There is no magic wand you can wave or pixie dust you can sprinkle over your business to take it on to the next level – instead you're going to need a combination of effective tools, systems and techniques working together, in harmony, to collectively transform how your business functions on every level – that's what's going to make it fly!

Don't worry, though, unlike an aircraft in flight, you don't need to get absolutely everything perfectly correct; success will come through an ongoing process of improvement and by focusing on the key success ingredients.

Evolution not revolution

Well-known companies are often in the news; it might be a major supermarket chain announcing that it's about to launch a new range of products or one major bank is taking over another major bank. These are significant announcements that companies are making all the time – if they weren't significant we wouldn't be hearing about them.

All this can give the impression that to grow your business you need to be making major, revolutionary changes all the time – don't be fooled, this is a completely false notion. The good news is that real, effective business change is achieved in nice, easy to apply, bite-sized steps and what's more, these little chunks of action are much easier to fit in to your already busy schedule. Even those momentous announcements are *nothing more than the coming together of a large number of small steps.*

Acceptance of this perspective is a significant first step in seeing business development as something that really is accessible for you. In fact, I'd like to go further and say you could take your very first bite-size step today, and then when you've taken that first step, take your next bite-size step tomorrow, and then keep it going and going... ongoing! ...Why not?

Action starts right here...

Reading and learning about the what and the how is a crucial starting point for strengthening and growing your business but as you're doing this – I mean starting right now! – you need to begin to, slowly and gently, develop your action plan. So, if you've not already done so, I'd like you to now keep a pen and a notebook to hand and as you *work* through this book, carefully consider what steps you can start taking to get moving in the right direction.

You should regard this as the very first step in the development of your business. Don't worry about trying to get your plans perfect first time – this almost never happens – accept that, as you go along you will be constantly reviewing and refining your plans and ideas. The changes that you will make should not be seen as corrections of errors, rather they are just a part of the constant stream of bite-sized steps you'll need to make in the ongoing process of business and personal growth.

And your first step would be?

Once more, ask yourself the question: if I were going to take action right now, what would be my first step?... and then what?

It's important to have clarity on this as soon as you resolve to do something – one of the most common reasons for procrastination is not having a clear idea on where to start.

In virtually all cases you can answer this question in a few seconds – a minute at the most! Once you've resolved this point then it's just a matter of deciding when and where.

Don't just apply this here... do it all the time... make it a habit. This mindful process of constantly seeking out action steps for making things happen will help to ensure that you continually keep your business and personal development moving along at a nice steady speed.

Be patient with yourself

If you're ambitious to take your business onto another level then it's likely you're itching to get going and take the world by storm! I would advocate a little caution here. It's important to be realistic about how much time you can allocate to growth, as this time may well be at the expense of short-term income and survival. Be careful to keep a sensible balance between the two.

It's also important to remember the key point I made earlier – that business success comes from getting a combination of things right in your business; no one single change is likely to bring you instant success. This developmental process takes a little time and requires your patience.

The savvy business owner is both patient and tenacious – they watch carefully to see what results from their actions – and recognise it's a learning, trial-and-error, process. The more you learn the better you get. It's an unwritten law and, if you work in harmony with it, it will pay you dividends.

Learn, learn, learn

If *you* don't develop and grow, the nature and quality of decisions you make will remain largely unchanged, so your business will not develop and grow. This is a vital point to take on board, right now; development can only take place in your business if you and the people you have around you are learning and developing.

Do not underestimate the significance of this. Now here's another hard fact to take on board...

> **The skills that got your business to where it is right now will not be enough to take you to the next level.**

To get different and better results you have to change what you're doing... sorry, there's no way around this one; it's just the way it is.

Business, like life I suppose, is a constant learning process – so if you really want to grow your business you need to acquire new skills in order to keep things moving forward. Some might well ask the question; at what point do I no longer need to learn? I think *you* already know what my answer's going to be, right?

So you need to accept as part of your way of thinking about your business, that from this point onwards you are on an ongoing journey of personal learning and development, and that doesn't only go for you as business owner, it also applies to those who work with you – yes, they will need to develop too – but for you, henceforth, try to view it as a way of life!

Winners and losers

The experiences of life are there for all of us to learn from and our ability to develop and grow is largely determined by our capacity to take on board those experiences and modify our actions accordingly.

I'm sure you can think of people you know who learn nothing from their experiences and become totally entrenched in their fixed views about the world in which they live.

You may meet someone you've not seen for several years but they've not changed a bit, a little older perhaps, but no wiser – still treading the same path, making the same errors getting ever more resentful at the bad breaks that life sends their way.

At the other extreme, there are canny individuals who are constantly learning from and adapting to their environment. They're observing, listening, growing and getting better; moving inexorably in the direction they want to go, no matter how painful the inevitable setbacks they experience along the way might be. No prizes for spotting which category the savvy small business owner falls into!

Success doesn't happen in a straight line

Expecting to start with the perfect idea, immediately develop the ideal plan, set out exactly the right steps and achieve everything you wish without any problems or changes along the way is seriously naïve. This simply never happens – life just doesn't work that way. You have to have failures along the way – it's how it works!

It's not an easy path from here to where you want to be – if it was that easy everyone would be successful – you will inevitably take some wrong turns; accept them as part of your learning process. Something you're about to try may not work but that should never stop you giving it your best shot.

> ### Be willing to try...
>
> Let's face it: carving a large piece of wood with a small blunt knife, made from a soft metal, in order to shape it into a thin round disk you might just be able to make roll, sounds like a lot of hard work based on nothing

> more than a hunch. Besides, at the end of all that work you may find that it just won't work the way you expect – so why bother?
>
> *Now doesn't that sound like a strong argument for **not** inventing the wheel?*

The success loop

You need to operate your business so that you constantly develop and learn from the things that inevitably go wrong. So when you set out your plans, accept at the outset that you may have to modify and refine them as you test what works and what doesn't.

If you think about it, there's a loop of action here; you try something new, you learn from what works and what doesn't work and modify and try again and then you monitor results and refine again and so on. *This is a success process – no failure involved – ignore the doubters!!!*

Listen and learn

The experiences and knowledge of others can be an invaluable source of learning as you move your business forward, but you need to watch out for the pitfalls…

Beware prophets of doom

Many times, over my career, have I come across individuals who will confidently advise you of the long list of reasons why what you're planning to do simply won't work. I'd try to devise a new approach to a particular problem and I'd be robustly informed: "You can't do that!" when often it was clear that my informant had not really taken any time at all to seriously consider the pros and cons. "OK" I'd say, "what if we changed this around or tweaked that..." only to get the response; "no, no, no".

This kind of negativity is, to say the least, frustrating, but more significantly, if it is allowed to influence your thinking, it can stifle creativity and undermine your confidence. Don't get me wrong I'm not for one moment advocating that you shouldn't seek the opinions of others; on the contrary, it's crucially important that you have one or more people you can bounce your ideas off, but you'll need to be discerning about the advice you get and how you use it.

People you trust

You should know from experience that there are certain people in your life whose counsel you can trust – perhaps they have relevant experience or they are known for giving carefully considered, well-balanced advice – these are the people you need to turn to. Run your ideas by them, make it clear that you trust their opinion and listen carefully to the logic of their arguments.

Don't be a sponge

Even the people you trust will have different views – do not make the fatal mistake of being overly influenced by the last person you spoke to – if you do that you'll find yourself constantly chopping and changing.

No one can fully understand you, your circumstances or what feels right to you, like you can. So when you receive advice or opinions, whatever the source, give careful consideration to how the logic of what you have been told stacks up with what you already know. Does it sound like good sense and is it consistent with what you already know to be true? If the answer is "yes" then ask yourself how you might test this new piece of information and, if appropriate, *assimilate* it into your strategy.

If there appear to be any flaws in the logic – examine these potential problems closely – remember, if a particular argument, on the face of it, doesn't appear to stack up it may well be because it really doesn't stack up!

Record what you resolve

It may seem like a chore but you really must ensure that you keep a record of the decisions you've made and the conclusions drawn. Always tidy up any meeting or discussion notes so they're easy to follow.

If you've just had a meeting, pass your notes back to those who took part and invite further thoughts and comments. Feedback is crucially important as we can all come up with significant refinements once we've had time to reflect.

Key points from this chapter

1. Start building your planning notes right now and then, as you build your knowledge, keep on refining them. It's an ongoing process; don't stop!

2. Focus first on giving yourself more time and then use it to create yourself even more time: you won't make progress unless you create that breathing space!

3. Be clear on what you want to achieve and what actions will get you there – anything else is a distraction!

4. Significant progress is nothing more the cumulative effect of a large number of small, bite-sized steps. How liberating is that? It means real business development is accessible to you!

5. Accept that you can't possibly achieve everything you want to; there are only so many hours in a day. Focus on what's most crucial for achieving what you want; that way the stuff that doesn't get done will always be the least important to you.

6. There's no one thing you can do to make your business a success; it's more about getting a combination of things right.

7. Each time you decide upon a course of action, ask yourself "What would be my first step?" Then ask yourself "OK, if I did that, what would be my second step?" By getting clarity immediately, it's much easier to maintain that forward momentum.

8. If you want your business to develop, you must seek to constantly develop and learn. Acquire your new knowledge from your own experiences and from others. Always be ready to listen to others but do so discerningly!

CHAPTER THREE

Taking hold

IT'S A SAD fact that many small businesses are completely rudderless, with their owners having no sense of direction, very often never even realising they need one. This is usually characterised by all plans, choices and decisions being made on a strictly short-term, day-to-day basis.

Of course, many of those routine decisions are important and necessary for the effective running of any business, but to focus exclusively on the short-term issues means the business is going nowhere.

To strengthen your business so it can survive in the face of any challenges, with the potential to take your business – and your life – in the direction you want to go, you have to take charge and accept the role of leader.

Revisiting your job description

What outstanding leaders do...

History has recorded the deeds of some truly inspirational military leaders: Alexander the Great, Saint Joan of Arc and Julius Caesar provide fine examples. In modern-day business we hear of such successful leaders as Bill Gates, Anita Roddick and Richard Branson, among many others. All of these individuals have been fabulously successful in their field – no doubt about it – but let's not place them on too high a pedestal; they've experienced many failures too.

Great business leaders are not infallible; they're not automatically super intelligent either. I'm not going to try to define these people in one short pithy phrase, that's not possible, but I can tell you that none of them get too bogged down in the day-to-day detail of their businesses; they focus on the longer term... the bigger picture. They have a clear vision of where they are at any point in time and where they want to be and concentrate on developing specific action steps for getting there.

These are undeniably common traits of effective leaders and you need keep this in mind if you wish for something better for your business.

The leadership myth

Leadership is something you're either born with or you're not – it's not something you can learn, right? Well, actually, no, that isn't right at all!

I'm not saying you can change yourself into an Alexander the Great or a Bill Gates – you don't need to be on that level to be highly successful in business. What I am saying is that effective leadership consists of a set of skills, many of which can be learnt quickly and easily. When these skills are effectively applied to your business, the difference it will make can take your breath away!

Let's be clear: effective leadership for your business is *definitely accessible to you* – but, if you're not making progress right now, you're going to need to make some changes.

Take me to your leader

Leadership of your business is about taking control, about making key decisions regarding the direction in which you're going and setting out the specific steps that will get you there. Management, on the other hand, is concerned with pulling together the necessary resources that that will bring those key steps to fruition.

Every successful business needs effective leadership and management – but these qualities are sadly lacking in many small businesses, with most owners focusing almost exclusively on the short-term operational stuff in an almost 100% *responsive* role.

The most common symptom of this is "crisis management" – you must have heard of this term – dealing first with one urgent matter that presents itself, and then taking a short breath before wading into the next urgent matter that lands on their plate. Planning? Forget it – they're far too busy handling the current crisis! Does this sound familiar? If it does and you want to break out of this you'll need to change the way you work.

So who's the leader in your business? If it's not you, then who? And who's providing strong management? If not you, then who? Oh, and by the way, if you have a direct competitor who's got their act together on all this stuff... look out!

So let's be clear – business success is not going to be achieved by just sticking to the day-to-day routine stuff – if you want to move on from where you are now, you need to stand back and take a look at that bigger picture.

Jack-of-all-trades

Leading and running your small business effectively means that you need to wear a number of different hats, requiring skills in three distinct areas:

1. *Technical Skills*

In order to deal with the daily routines you need the fundamental technical skills to do whatever is required to serve your customers and operate your business. This is the stuff we see all businesses doing: mending a roof, laying carpets, making deliveries. You need the skills to do this: how else can you serve your customers?

2. *Management Skills*

At the next level you need to manage the resources that enable you to carry out all that day-to-day stuff for the right customers, in the right way, in the right place, with the right resources and at the right time. If the roofer, for instance, doesn't make sure roof tiles are delivered on the right day he won't be able to start work on those roof repairs.

3. *Leadership Skills*

*As the saying goes; the technician is the one who produces it, the manager manages the processes of producing it and the leader is the person who decides what **it** is. In other words, it's the leader's job to take the longer-term view and decide what products and services the business will provide, now and in the future. He'll also need to determine what changes will need to be made in order to achieve all this and how it's all going to be pulled together.*

Where do you fit in?

Are you a technician, manager or a leader? The truth is that there's something of all three in every one of us but usually one of these is the dominant characteristic.

Many people, though not all, start their business with the aim of making full use of the technical skills they already have. That's fine to start with but, as already discussed, if you want to grow your business you need to develop a broader range of skills.

What's more, leadership skills can save you pots of time by providing you a clear direction and sense of purpose, thus allowing you to make consistent decisions that support each other and provide a cumulative positive force for taking you in the direction you want to go.

A word about entrepreneurs

You will no doubt have heard of famous, high-flying business owners who risk large sums of money on big deals that can, and sometimes do, generate massive profits. Many of these big deals, however, will fail spectacularly causing eye-watering losses.

Such people tend to be more comfortable with the greater levels of risk that go with those potentially higher rewards: and this can lead to a more adventurous and less financially inhibited approach. They'll still face the same challenges as any other business owner but additionally they'll need to develop skills in negotiating and deal-making, properly assessing the risks they take and acquiring appropriate finance.

In essence an entrepreneur will expend most of their time on leadership activities and is unlikely to get too involved in day-to-day technical or management work.

If you're seeking to take an entrepreneurial approach to your business, once you've got your strong foundations in place, your next step should be to develop your skills in these areas. For more on this refer to *Further Reading* at the end of this book.

Decisions – upping your game

During the course of any busy working day you're faced with countless decisions. These range in importance from choosing how many pencils to order from the stationers to determining your key objectives for the next five years.

Of course, when it comes to making the really important decisions, we want to make all the right moves but that's not easy in a world where we don't always have complete information. You seldom know, with absolute certainty, how events in the environment in which you operate can affect your business and the decisions you're about to make.

If that's not bad enough there's the creeping self-doubt – am I making the right choice here; what if this happens? What if that doesn't work as I expect? For some people this can cause serious prevarication, to the point where ultimately they end up doing nothing at all. At best, in these situations, a great deal of time can be wasted through repeatedly weighing up the pros and cons of every choice you make.

Even if you're reasonably decisive in the way you work there's still the danger that your decision making is inconsistent – thus generating courses of action that work against each other. This reduces your effectiveness and wastes a huge amount of your time and effort.

Your ever present compass

How much easier would life be, then, if you had, constantly at hand, a decision-making framework to help you make those key choices in your business? How much simpler would your decision making be if you had a ready-made set of criteria that you could refer to at any time, giving greater clarity on, and confidence in, the choices you make? Well you *can* have this and here's how…

Getting a sense of direction

Getting from here to wherever it is you want to be, means that you need to be congruent in *all* your decision making.

> **All your strategies, plans and actions…**
> **…the very way you think…**
> **…need to be geared up to taking you…**
> **…and your business in the direction you want to go.**

If you're not operating consistently then the positive effects of the key decision you made this week can easily be undermined and even completely negated by a decision you made last week. If you don't believe this can happen, just look at the way successive governments work. Forget party politics, they all do it; setting up new policies today which they ditch just a few months down the road.

And you need clarity...

If you have a clear vision of where you want to be then you have a point of reference for setting out your plans for the future and, indeed, for making your day-to-day decisions and choices. By having a decision-making "touchstone", like this, you can give yourself a much easier and clearer route to consistently smarter moves.

What's more you'll take less time making those decisions, you'll prevaricate less and afterwards you'll feel more comfortable about the choices you've made. That feeling of greater certainty will, crucially, give you increased confidence as you continue to take your business forward.

So you need a *charter* or framework for making consistent choices. Here's a nice, simple way to develop just that: three short, sharp lists providing you with criteria for all your key decisions...

List #1: Where do you want to be?

Let's simplify the question by asking: where do you see yourself in three years' time? Note I'm talking about *you* here, not your business.

OK, take a sheet of paper and make some notes in answer to the following questions:

1. *What's most important to you? Spouse, family, career, money/ income, lifestyle, property ownership, health, retirement, leisure time... what? Make a list and rank the items in order of importance.*
2. *For each of these consider what changes you'd like to see in your life over the next three years.*
3. *Keep the list for future reference.*

List #2: How can your business help?

Based on the above list, set out some criteria for your business – using three years as your target period. Here's what these might include:

1. *What level of profits will your business need to generate? Try to set yourself a specific goal here – don't worry about getting this right first time: you can refine as you go. However, aim for some consistency with the personal income aspirations you've set out in list #1.*

2. *What products/services will your business provide and to whom?*

3. *How will these be positioned – high quality or cheap and cheerful?*

4. *How big will your business need to be in terms of sales volume, number of employees and size of business premises? Once again you may find it helpful to hang specific numbers on this: don't worry if you get it wrong at this stage, you can refine as you go.*

5. *Where will you operate your business from?*

6. *What will be your role within the business?*

7. *What new skills will you need?*

8. *Keep the list for future reference.*

Do not consider this an exhaustive list; if something occurs to you later that's not included, feel free to add it.

List #3: What about your values?

Where do you stand on the following?

1. *Are you looking for the "quick buck" or do you seek to build strong, lasting, long-term working relationships with your customers?*

2. *How should you treat your employees? Do you want to help them develop and grow in their roles and their lives?*

3. *What about your dealings with your suppliers and trading partners – what kind of relationships best serve your needs?*

4. *Do you want to just get along with the outside world as best you can or would you prefer to proactively build a positive reputation?*

5. *Would you like to give something back to the community?*

6. *What other issues do you feel strongly about that you wish your business to stand for?*

7. *Keep the list for future reference.*

Take a break

Leave it at least a couple of days and then carry out a brief review of your three lists to make sure you've not changed your mind on any points and that all items are compatible. Keep it realistic, for instance tripling the size of your business and staying hands on might not be compatible with four months' holiday a year!

Anything else you'd like to change, take out or add?

Voilà! – your decision-making framework

Your new lists relating to your personal aspirations, your supporting business goals and your fundamental values will now provide you with your "touchstone" for making all your future key choices. From now on, whenever you're faced with an important decision to make, refer to these lists – if a new idea or strategy doesn't fit or is in some way intrinsically inconsistent with the framework you've set out then you're going to need a very good reason for going ahead with it!

One final point – keep your framework current and relevant by regularly reviewing it and making sure your aspirations, goals and values still hold. Changing them is OK, they're not carved in stone, but if you do make a change, just make sure you're doing it for the right reasons.

Save yourself even more time

Once you've completed your lists you might wish, once again, to review the items in "Avoiding the time wasters" in Chapter 2. In light of your new aims and values you should find even more scope for cutting out work activities that don't fit!

Joined-up thinking

You can provide yourself with an even more comprehensive decision-making framework by gradually defining specific goals consistent with your vision and values.

The next logical step is to further break down your goals into more detailed, specific, action steps – providing an easy-to-follow trail from your overall *vision* to what happens when the rubber hits the road. Can you see how each level in your planning provides the context for the next level of detail? *Now that's joined-up thinking*!

What's more, if you were now to pull all this into one single document you'd have at your fingertips a comprehensive framework for making consistent, well considered decisions in *every* aspect of your business... What you'd also have is a *business plan...*

A plan for your business

What's most important for you here is that you are totally in control of your business: in terms of where it's going (your vision); how you're going to go about your business (your values); your overarching plans for taking you from where you are to where you want to be; and breaking your plans down into specific action steps that will, in turn, support and promote all of this.

A single, short, sharp document that pulls all this together, where you can review and adapt it as necessary, will help you massively to get a real grip on your business... and your life!

You don't need to take a standard textbook approach to develop your plan – you can lay it out in any format you like – just so long as it feels comfortable, FOR YOU, to work with and IT KEEPS YOU IN CONTROL. I've seen someone use a single page document that worked just fine for him!

OK, let me get a bit a more specific here; as you work through this book and accumulate your notes I'd suggest you start to organise them into the following categories:

Your *business plan...*

1. Your vision

2. Your values

3. Your business and personal income goals

4. Other goals, eg growth in sales, number of customers, number of employees, etc

5. Plans that will achieve your goals, including:

   a. Marketing

   b. Production and delivery of your products and services

   c. Finance

   d. Admin

   e. People *(recruiting, training, etc)*

   f. Anything else that you feel is important

6. Your detailed action steps for making all this happen

7. Your process for checking, from time to time, that it's all working together as you'd hoped and for taking corrective action where required

Don't try to pour huge amounts of your time in setting all this up – it's not necessary! Just record what you learn, capture your thoughts and arrange your ever-improving notes under the above headings.

To get going all you need to do is set up a sheet of A4 paper with one of each of the above headings at the top of the page and then, as you go along, insert your thoughts, ideas, plans, etc.

I'd also suggest that, from time to time you review and refine your notes – making them shorter, more concise as you go – and make sure, above all, that your planned actions are consistent and serve to reinforce each other.

Let's be clear: *this is not about doing anything extra* in your business development; it's about intelligently organising the whole process – overall this is a real timesaver!

Different things to different people…

Clients of ours, having made a small business loan application, have often asked me for help because their bank manager has requested a *business plan*. What they're usually really asking for here is some kind of profit or cash-flow forecast.

To a potential investor, or a lender of significantly large sums of money, the business plan becomes a more comprehensive document: in addition to profit and cash projections for several years ahead, it will provide details of the strengths and weaknesses of the business plus an assessment of the strategic opportunities open to it as well as the significant potential threats that lay ahead.

If, at some point in the future, you are applying to an investor or a lender you may well have to provide such a detailed document. When that happens you'll be able to pull much of the information you need for this from your own, less formal plan and confidently demonstrate that you have a tight control on your business.

Your decision-making toolkit

Faced with a constant flow of important choices to make you can sometimes feel overwhelmed particularly when you encounter a complicated problem. You'll be relieved to learn then that there are a number of techniques you can apply to help you solve problems, particularly where you're having trouble getting your head around them:

1. **Write it down**

   Sometimes the issues you're facing can be so complex that you really need to work your way through the ins and outs. A useful technique is to literally argue with yourself: suggest a way forward then play devil's advocate and look for problems with it – toss it around and properly air all the pros and cons, keeping a written record of your thinking as you go.

   This approach will help you to clearly define the problem and as you do this you'll naturally start to think about ways to solve it. Another advantage here is that you're continually recording your thinking, this way you don't forget how you drew your conclusions on a particular point and, just as important, you don't lose your good ideas. This will also mean that, if you have to come back to it, you can review where you were when last you looked at it and then quickly get started on further developing your thinking from there.

2. **The helicopter view**

   Getting a grip on a problem can often be made easier by viewing the whole thing in one place; on one sheet of paper, for instance. This can easily be achieved by representing the problem in the form of a diagram or map.

   One major advantage of this approach is that by using arrows and connecting lines it's much easier to recognise related issues and get a deeper overall understanding of the problem.

   Maps are a key part of my working toolkit and I use them not only for problem solving but also for planning meetings and even the composing of complicated business letters. True they don't suit everyone but if you're a visual thinker you might want to give these a try. Tony Buzan is an author who has written much on the topic of Mind Maps; for more on this see Further Reading at the end of this book.

3. **Imagine you're explaining it to someone**
Picture yourself looking for help from one of your peers. Now explain to them the nature of the problem in detail. Assume this person has absolutely no knowledge of the problem. Detail the challenges you face and why you feel your current approach will or will not work. Explain to this imaginary person every detail and all your concerns. As you do this note down any new ideas or concerns that occur to you and add these to your map/notes.

One variant is to imagine you're giving a talk to a group of people – using your imagination in this way can really help to stimulate your thinking.

A further aid in this process is to try and explain it as if it were a story, introducing the sequence of events that have brought you to where you are and taking it all the way through to the ending you require – imagining ways that will get to that ending.

Some people find it helpful to literally stand up and speak to do this. There's nothing wrong with this but should you decide to try it out it's probably best done when there's no one else around – you don't want people to think you've lost your marbles!.

Barristers do it!

A number of our clients who are legal barristers, based in the Temple in central London, have told me that before presenting their case they'll get clarity on the right approach by imagining they're already right there in the courtroom laying out their case. They will literally stand up, while alone in their room in chambers, and present out loud the details of their case as if they were in the courtroom – testing how the content and delivery of the arguments will work. The fact that this approach is continually used is real-life proof of its effectiveness.

---

4. ***Bounce it around***

   Discuss with your colleagues, spouse, friends – whomever – lobby opinion particularly on sticking points just to get a different perspective.

   In order to ensure that you effectively explain the nature of the problem you might use the previous approach in combination with this one.

   This is a really important resource that is too often overlooked. OK, I accept if you're dealing with a highly technical subject then you're somewhat restricted in whom you can turn to for intelligent and appropriate input, but if you've been involved in a particular area of work for some time you must know someone who's facing similar challenges who you can toss this problem around with. If you don't, try to build contacts through networking, or signing up to appropriate forums on the web or joining a relevant institute or society and attending meetings and getting to know people who do what you do.

   If it's non-technical then it's almost certain that absolutely anyone can get you to look at a problem from an angle you hadn't considered.

   Try not to dismiss out of hand the ideas of someone who's looking over your shoulder at the problem for the first time: a fresh point of view might be just what you need.

Ideas from left field

In a large company I worked for, Stuart, a colleague of mine, was so desperate to find a solution to a management problem he had that he'd discuss it with anyone who would listen.

The trouble was his fellow team members had received the same training and had the same work background he had – so they were all coming at the problem from more or less the same angle.

Then, one evening when he was working late, he was sitting at his desk when in walked a young man employed by a contract cleaning company to empty the waste baskets. Stuart thought "why not" so he bounced the problem off the young man who, right off the top of his head came up with a number of random and somewhat unfocused ideas, one of which, would you believe it, ultimately led to an excellent solution.

An interesting lesson for the whole team and one I never forgot!

5. Don't rush it: plan it!

Many small business owners tend to make snap decisions and then just wade in. Sometimes this is because of genuine time pressures and other times it's because of an irrational need to just do something.

Planning is largely a cerebral activity with not much to show for it and thus the urge for physical action can be overwhelming. But you need to be clear that planning is the most important part of the whole process – no question!

If your physical efforts are taking you in the wrong direction then they have no value. When you don't plan, then your actions amount to little more than floundering around in the dark. If you do achieve your goals this way then it will be more by good luck than good judgment.

TIME OUT!

In his book *Making it Happen: Reflections on Leadership* Sir John Harvey-Jones recalls his time as managing director of ICI, when his UK operation set about building a new factory at the same time that a similar plant was to be built in Japan.

The Japanese, he recalls, were much slower at getting started with construction because they spent far more time meticulously planning out every aspect and contingency of the project – whereas their British counterparts needed to see action quickly and the project management team in charge was under pressure to show something tangible, in short order.

Not surprisingly, the UK operation was, apparently, off the blocks much faster. So you can imagine their dismay when the Japanese team came from behind and finished ahead of schedule and a long way ahead of their British counterparts.

Sir John lamented that lack of front-end planning and learnt the lesson.

6. Don't over-analyse

I've stressed the dangers of failing to plan before you take action but you also need to beware of the dangers of over-analysing You must have heard the term "analysis paralysis". This is, very likely, a term wryly coined by those who have fallen foul of their attempts to achieve that elusive "perfect plan".

Please believe me when I tell you: there is no such thing as a perfect business plan. It doesn't matter how thorough you are in your planning there'll always be something you either missed or could never have predicted. As your project progresses new dynamics will enter the picture and unforeseen new developments will inevitably arise. Don't worry, it's not your fault, it's how it works! When this happens you just adapt your plans accordingly.

When you're at the point when you're sure you've covered all the key bases, you need to jump in and start taking hard action. Once you're at this stage, quit worrying about whether you're ready or not and start getting some forward motion.

Remember, planning doesn't stop when the action starts but it does change: now your planning will be focused on dealing with the ever changing dynamics of your project. Do not fear this – accept it as a natural part of the process.

7. Don't forget your compass!

Always be mindful of what it is you're aiming to achieve both in terms of your aims and your values – this will provide you with that all-important framework for incisive, confident decision making.

Your ever evolving business plan will provide you with further, more detailed guidance and a greater underlying feeling of certainty about the direction in which your difficult decisions should be taking you. Let your compass be your guide, and your conscience, and it will serve you well!

8. The massive power of combination

No one technique is automatically better than another: the methods you apply will depend largely upon what works for you and what best fits with the challenges you face.

Speaking for myself, I always like to take that helicopter view, at least to start with, by mapping out the problems so that, as I go along, I can quickly review all the key issues and see how all the elements interrelate. In combination with this I'll write (or type) detailed linear notes on any particularly sticky issues and discuss, with those whose counsel I trust, possible solutions along with their attendant pros and cons. If that fails to provide a solution then I'll resort to one or a combination of the other methods.

Key points from this chapter

1. Feel the need to lead! As owner of your business you need to provide clarity of direction and steer a steady course. The benefits of taking a lead are immense in terms of time saved and the powerful cumulative effect of all decisions and actions pointing in the same direction.

2. Decision making – do it better, do it quicker. Make lists of your personal aspirations, what your business will need to look like in order to help you to achieve them and of the values that will determine how you will do business in the future. These lists will provide you with a powerful framework for making quicker, better quality choices.

3. For more detailed control in all your decision making, allow your *business plan* to gradually build and evolve and then let it be your guide. Keep your plan short and to the point.

4. Use effective tools for making the right choices. You don't have to be a natural leader to make better quality choices; you just need to use the right techniques for the job. Make life easier for yourself by following methods used by those who've already been there.

CHAPTER FOUR

What your customers want

HAVE YOU ever considered who the most important person in your business is? Just take one minute to think about it now?

Done that? OK. Now, for the moment just park those thoughts and consider the following line of argument:

The profits you make now and in the future will depend, largely, on the sales you make. You can only make sales if you are meeting your customers' needs and making sure your customers and potential customers know it. You do this through effective communication of the benefits of buying your products and services and of the relevance of those benefits to your target audience.

Equally important is that you deliver (at least) or over deliver (preferably) on those promises, so that those who buy from you will want to come back for more and will recommend you to others.

Of course you need to control your costs but key to both short- and long-term profit growth is profitable sales growth.

In short, your ability to increase profits will ultimately be determined by how well you serve your customers. If you completely fail to focus your business on this, you have no chance of enjoying any real business growth.

So, I come back to my original question: who is the most important person in your business?

That's right, *it's your customer*!

Marketing actually

Given what I've been banging on about, I expect you saw this coming, right? Whether you're really ambitious and want to grow your business, or you're seeking to do nothing more than survive, you'll need to build your plans around the wants, needs, aspirations and concerns of your customers, as well as the challenges they face and the solutions they seek.

Serving your customers – past, present and future – is absolutely central to the very existence of your business. *Marketing activities,* which are dedicated to serving your customers well, should therefore be *central* to all your business activities. This means, therefore, that *marketing considerations should pervade every aspect of your business.*

Let's look at this statement a little closer...

✓ *You want your business to make a profit? That means you have to sell products or services. So you'll need to develop **selling techniques.***

✓ *Effective selling techniques – ones that actually sell your products or services and encourage customers to come back time and time again – will need to be carefully thought through; that's where **marketing** comes in.*

✓ *Your sales team may be good at what they do and the techniques they use may be effective but if customers aren't coming through the door in the first place (literally and figuratively) then your selling resources are wasted. So you've got to inform people you're there and of the benefits of the products or services you sell – that's where* **marketing** *comes in.*

✓ *If you want to have any credibility with your customers then you need to make sure that your products and services really do meet* **their** *needs and that you* **always** *deliver on your promises. That means looking at the fundamentals of whatever it is you produce: what qualities do your products and services need to have in order to meet customer requirements? You need to make sure you know the answer to this crucial question – that's where* **marketing** *comes in.*

✓ *The production and distribution of your products and services are also crucially important in serving your customers. You need to be aware of how you should arrange your production process (or service delivery) and therefore serve your customers with what they need, when and where they need it – that's where* **marketing** *comes in.*

✓ *After-sales services say a great deal about the integrity of any business but how should you organise this and what should your policy be with regard to returns, replacements, free repairs, guarantees, etc? That's where* **marketing** *comes in.*

✓ *You may think that back-office admin, such as bookkeeping, invoicing, credit-control, managing the money, purchasing, wages admin and paying the bills cannot possibly be affected by marketing – you'd be wrong. All of these, in a variety of ways, communicate to the outside world how you do what you do – and if you want everyone out there to trust you, you need to be consistent all the way down the line. Also, most of these functions include some communications with customers and you need* **all** *customers' dealings with your business to be 100% consistent, always leaving a favourable and positive impression – that's where* **marketing** *comes in.*

Because your key focus has to be your customers, *marketing must be central to all your business planning, decisions and activities.* Your production and service delivery, for instance, is crucially important but if your customers don't want what you're producing, you're wasting your time.

Is all this a bit of shock?

I expect some people might have a little difficulty taking this one on board, particularly those with a technical background – I count myself in this category. It's certainly true that most people setting up their business from scratch will indeed come from that technical or production perspective. You know how it works: you have a particular skill and you conclude that you can set up your own business using that key strength.

This approach is fine when you're just getting your business started but if you're looking for long-term survival and growth, you'll need to move away from just producing something that you hope people will buy – and take specific action to *ensure* that you know what they're looking for and what their needs are – and these are things that continually change.

TIME OUT!

Let's keep some perspective here. The current context is business growth in general and business profit growth in particular. In times when the very survival of your business is under serious threat, then of course, marketing issues must, temporarily, step into the background in order to leave all required resources available to deal with those threats. Once the crisis is over and you've set plans in motion for averting or reducing your vulnerability to such threats then, and only then, should you consider stepping back into *development mode.*

First among equals

As well as planning for marketing, you'll need to lay out your plans for production (and/or service delivery), sales administration, after-sales services, finance, as well as managing, motivating and remunerating your people… and the list goes on.

So here's a key point to take on board… While marketing is key and will pervade the whole business, you must be clear that *all activities are equally important.*

It may sound like a contradiction when I say all plans are equal while at the same time arguing that the marketing plan is where you start and all other plans should support it. However you can't market your products if you haven't got a plan for making them or a plan for raising finance to lease that factory unit you need.

Indeed your marketing plan may have to be modified because you can't get the finance you need to purchase some crucial piece of equipment; this interdependence of each of the strategies is a real leveller. So the bottom line here is: to make any new project work, *all* elements of your plans must work together – if they don't, it all fails!

Let's now look at some crucially important criteria for checking that your new marketing ideas will work…

Watching out for the other stuff

Let's say your research has identified a large market for a product you could develop. While potential sales could be very high there are other important matters you'll need to consider before you jump in…

✓ *How profitable will it be? In other words: is it really worth doing? So many times have I seen traders jump into markets with potential for high sales volumes only to find that profit margins are abysmally low. Where this occurs it will inevitably mean that sales volumes will need to be extremely high in order to make even reasonable profits.*

✓ Can you afford it? How much will it cost to do this and have you the cash available? If not, is it possible to get finance? How much will the finance cost (interest charges, arrangement fees, renewal fees, etc)? If you can't raise the funds then your plan has fallen at the first fence.

✓ How well does it fit in with your existing activities? Will it make use, for instance, of existing equipment, expertise, marketing techniques or channels of distribution? If so it's likely you'll find it much easier to get started and you may benefit from significant cost savings. If you're answering "No" to each of these then you need to be clear on what the true strengths of your planned project really are.

✓ Does it work to your strengths? A lucrative heating service contract opportunity that your effective marketing activities have generated may seem enticing but if you have zero expertise in that area you need to be clear on just how feasible your plans are.

✓ Does it contribute to the achievement of your vision and your long-term objectives? If the answer is no then you need to think very seriously about why it is you are considering going "off-piste".

✓ Is it compatible with your values? If you've already thought these through carefully (see Chapter 3) why would you consider an activity that takes you outside the scope in which you wish to operate?

No question, when you're setting out your business plans, marketing is where you should start but you must not overlook other crucially important criteria. Always take a balanced view before you commit.

Your four key marketing aims

Moving forward with your marketing development is going to be so much easier if you have clarity on what it is you're supposed to be doing. How do you convert your sales growth goals into a specific, clear and congruent set of steps that, in concert, maximise your chances of success? More immediately: Where do you start?

OK, let's take a look at your main marketing aims... Whatever marketing technique you use, it will fall into one or more of the four following categories:

1. **Making first contact**

   Often referred to as "lead generation", this first step in building relationships with your customers has to be aimed at letting them know you're there, what you're offering and what benefits there are to them in buying from you.

   You need to make that first contact so you can start some form of dialogue or interaction as a first step to making that crucial first sale with each customer – but the techniques here are not about making the sale, rather they are about making that first vital communication that will give you the opportunity to demonstrate the benefits of your wares.

2. **Making that first sale**

   Here we are looking at techniques and tools for effectively communicating to your prospective customer the key benefits of the products or services you offer (note the overlap here with the previous category) *and, perhaps, to get them to buy. Remember, you only get an opportunity to apply these techniques if you've been successful in the previous lead generation stage.*

   Effective techniques will favourably influence prospective customers, even if they do not convert into an immediate sale – initially the process may achieve nothing more than a strengthening of the relationship with your customers or prospective customers – this will, at the very least, contribute to a pipeline of business for the future.

   *Of course, it would be naïve to expect that every technique you employ will work every time: prospective customers will respond to your messages in different ways. As any salesman will tell you: **it's a numbers game** and the more relevant people you're getting your powerful messages to, the more you'll succeed.*

3. Getting your customers to come back

What's the difference between a customer and a client? Answer: a client is a customer who buys from you time and time again. Customers are great… clients are better!

It's a well-known fact that it's much less costly to sell again to a satisfied customer than to sell for the first time to someone who has never heard of your products or services. For this reason you'll need to have techniques in place for maintaining relationships with clients and promoting loyalty to your brand of products or services.

Some marketing specialists refer to loyal customers as the "goldmine". This may sound an exaggeration but in truth if you're successfully fulfilling the needs or solving the problem of your customers then, of course, they will keep coming back for more – and the income you generate from this is costing you nothing in terms of marketing expenditure, time and effort.

Techniques for building long-term relationships – often referred to as "customer retention" – in this way are crucially important and deserve a significant portion of your marketing efforts.

4. Selling more to each customer

In theory you can maximise sales from your "goldmine" by applying techniques aimed at encouraging your clients to buy from you on a more frequent basis and/or by buying more each time they do.

Of course, you'll need to be careful not to over-egg the pudding here. A common error, especially for retail-oriented businesses is to hard sell and constantly badger those customers listed on its database – which may well annoy them and undermine that loyal relationship.

Correctly managed, the process of regularly communicating with your clients for mutual benefit can work well for everyone. If you're aiming to achieve a healthy balance between maximising your sales in the short-term and gradually growing your sales for the medium and long-term then you'll need to be directing your efforts at all four of your key marketing aims in combination.

A balanced approach

I'd recommend, given the limited resources of most small businesses, that the smart move would be to gradually build up a combination of marketing techniques that simultaneously address all four key goals in your marketing framework.

The good news here is that many techniques can apply equally to lead generation as well as sales conversion and repeat sales – so once you start to develop these techniques they can, in combination, provide a very powerful force for growth in your business.

Savvy ground rules

If you're going to market your products and services effectively you'll need to understand some foundational principles that will set the scene for all your thinking...

There's no substitute for a great product...

As you may have noticed, the subject of marketing is strongly associated with the art of presentation and there can be no doubt that this is extremely important for the success of your business.

However, there's *no better marketing* tool for your business than a great product or service. If you want your customers to keep coming back for more, you have to deliver on your promises... and then some. If you tell them your product has certain benefits then it really does need to have those benefits.

If you don't deliver, then the best you can hope for is that they'll come back and complain – so you get a second chance. At worst they don't come back and complain, they don't come back at all. Ever. All human relationships are built on trust – this is crucially important – and if you fail to deliver on your promises, people don't always point it out, *but they always know!*

If you believe you can persistently let people down and get away with it you're deluding yourself. Come on, you know how it works – if you don't know me at all when you buy from me for a first time and I let you down badly, what are the chances you'll trust me enough in the future to buy from me again? That's human nature, right? As business owners we all know this but, for some reason, it's a life principle that's too often ignored.

Add value

"What's value?" This is a common question whenever I talk about adding value with clients. Value is the total benefit you bestow as part of the product or service you provide in return for what your customer is paying you.

"Benefit" is pretty much the operative word. You may offer a cuddly toy with every widget you sell, but the local company that assembles machines that use your widgets probably doesn't have much call for cuddly toys, so there's not much value there. OK that's an extreme example I admit, but you get the point, right? The real value of the benefits you provide is determined by the relevance they have to your customers and how they perceive them.

The bottom line here is: you need to provide a great product or service first and then accompany it with a powerful message that ensures the relevant audience is made fully aware of the real value being offered. It therefore follows that the more value you can add, the more attractive and different your overall offering (or proposition) is to your potential customers – and that's going to improve your chances of grabbing their attention.

Wrap it all in a great service

No matter how rich in value your products or services might be there will always be scope for adding even more value and benefits with the services that accompany them. This is also an area where there are a huge number of opportunities to impress your customers and prospective customers and to differentiate your business even more from your competitors.

If you want to improve your product or service "wrapper" you need to consider:

- ✓ How you can make it easier for your customers to:
  - Contact you
  - Find the products and services they need
  - Obtain your products or services in the most convenient way
  - Get what they need from you faster – if speed is important to them
- ✓ What can you add on to how you deliver your products or services?
- ✓ What after-sales services can you provide?
- ✓ What's the most positive way you can deal with complaints and problems?
- ✓ What guarantees can you provide?
- ✓ How can you learn from your mistakes and, therefore, constantly improve what you do?

This should not be considered an exhaustive list – try to seek out your own opportunities for adding value in this area and find something new and different that you can do for your customers.

It's not about the money

When I start talking about marketing with a client for the very first time, they invariably jump to the conclusion that I'm about to suggest they start spending money on advertising. I'd therefore like to make it clear from the outset, what I'm about to discuss has little to do with advertising or spending your money. In fact, it's more about spending – or should I say *investing* – your time.

If you're truly serious about growing your business you'll need to put time into your marketing. A significant element of which will need to be devoted to understanding your customers, their needs, gearing up your products and services accordingly and communicating the benefits of buying from you.

It's not a one-off project

You need to look upon your marketing activities as something you start now and continue to develop on an ongoing basis. It really is a never-ending process. If you're going to approach marketing in the right frame of mind then you not only need to accept this underlying principle without reservation – you must embrace it!

Beware the stop-start trap

One very common error made by service businesses, particularly where the main service is labour intensive, is to carry out just enough marketing to keep the staff busy for now.

This is characterised by short bursts of frenetic marketing activity, which bring in new business, followed by all resources being switched to dealing with the work that the marketing activities have generated – meaning, for a time, no marketing effort and, therefore, no new business is coming in. Eventually work runs out and thus another session of frenetic marketing activity ensues – and so the cycle continues.

At best, with luck, the business that follows this approach just about keeps its head above water but in the event of a sudden downturn in the market, it becomes vulnerable and it may then be necessary to lay off staff in order to survive. Trying to turn your flow of new business on and off like a tap is a risky approach and it is, by its very nature, *designed to avoid real growth.*

Of course, it's easy to fall into the trap of taking your foot off the marketing pedal at times when you're feeling too busy to cope but, if you are going to continue to steadily grow your business you'll need to plan for those additional workloads that come with underlying growth, not avoid them!

Your marketing mean machine

One golden rule referred to by marketing experts is the view that, if you are really serious about building your business then you should seek to build a *comprehensive set of techniques* for acquiring new customers and selling to them. These methods, working in combination, will drive your business forward and provide you with a broader range of options for dealing with problems and challenges in the future. Another key point here is that your business risk is reduced by having a multiplicity of technique options, should any one particular technique suddenly become less effective.

Most small businesses operate no more than one or two proven techniques for generating sales at any time – I'd suggest you should be constantly seeking out new techniques that work well for you and your business. If you're looking for real growth in your business, you'll need to gradually build up your arsenal of these techniques.

Hands up!

I once attended a seminar for local small businesses given by a marketing specialist who asked all 30-odd attendees to raise their right hand. He then asked for everyone who currently had in place two or more effective techniques for growing their business, to keep their hands in the air and the rest of us to put our hands down. About half of our number dropped their hands.

"If you use three or more effective techniques..." he went on, "...please keep your hand raised, the rest, please lower your hand." By the time he got to "four or more" techniques there was only one person with his hand still raised.

"If you're really serious about growing your business," he pointed out, "I'd suggest you need at least *EIGHT* effective techniques in place at any one time."

Don't be dismayed if you're currently nowhere near this, but don't ignore this shortfall either. Take it as a signal that you now need to start building your repertoire of effective techniques. If you're gradually working in that direction and you're making steady progress then, for now, you can accept you're doing enough. Just make sure, at the same time, you're constantly looking for new ways to build your momentum.

Once again I would counsel an approach of taking bite-sized steps. If you're not currently making as much progress as you would like, start doing marginally more on this. Monitor the progress you've made as a result of your new input; is it taking you where you want to go? If not, then, once more, seek out the next marginal step you can take – and build up that momentum gradually.

If you're feeling stretched and can't find the time, forget marketing development for a short while and work on yourself in order to free up that time (see Chapter 2 for help). Once you've achieved this you can revert back to building your marketing momentum.

Considering your position

If you've thoroughly carried out your research you should have a fairly clear idea of who your target customers are. But before you start to plan just how you're going to communicate with them, you need to be clear how you wish to position yourself in the market in which you operate.

Let's start by considering where you are now? Are your products and services at the cheap-and-cheerful end of the market, Rolls Royce high-quality variety, or somewhere in-between?

What about the way you deal with your potential customers? How will you conduct your communications? Will you seek to keep discussions brief to save time and resources or will you look to position yourself (or your sales team) as the trusted adviser who's there to provide prospective customers with even-handed professional guidance that adds value and builds trust.

There are arguments in favour of both positions but you need to be clear which way you want to go and be confident that, whatever choices you make on these matters, you're staying consistent with your goals and values.

It's worth bearing in mind that it's not so easy to grow your business or your income in the long run if your offering is of the cheap-and-cheerful variety. There are two key reasons for this. First, if you're competing on price alone then your profit margins will tend to be thin, meaning your profits will need to come from higher sales volumes and this brings with it a higher level of underlying risk. Second, lower prices tend to appeal more to those customers whose prime concern is price – so there's a much lower tendency towards any kind of brand loyalty. These customers will buy from you if you're cheaper, because you're cheaper – if someone comes along with an even lower-priced offer, more often than not they'll defect... without hesitation.

The most effective route to growth is building loyalty through an increased belief among your customers that your products and services are in some way intrinsically more attractive: by offering more benefits that are relevant to them and by doing it differently.

It wouldn't be fair to say you can't substantially build a business based on a competitive price strategy – there are many real life examples of a successful low pricing strategy but it is a tougher approach to take and it can bring with it greater risk. For more on this please refer to *The anatomy of business profit* in Chapter 6.

Another factor to consider is whether you'll maintain a simple, vanilla approach to what you offer for the price you charge or will you seek to constantly add value and differentiate your products?

The language of "benefits"

One of my first steps when I started to develop a marketing strategy for my own accountancy practice was to survey how other accountancy firms promoted themselves in their marketing literature. It became clear at a fairly early stage that most firms at that time were pretty clueless as to what might catch the attention of prospective clients. Typically, the home page of the web site would say:

✓ *We are accountants*

✓ *We've got x years' experience in tax*

✓ *We've been in practice for x years*

✓ *We've got these qualifications…*

Depressingly, the supporting pages of the site say more or less the same thing, just in more detail. As I relate this I can feel myself stifling a yawn!

Take my word for it this is absolutely not going to capture the attention of prospective customers – no way. Sure, this stuff is important and it should be made available to prospective clients when they're ready to look at it but it's not what pops their cork!

Let's face it, when you're looking to buy something, whatever it is, you're asking yourself "What's in it for me?" In other words, what are the benefits to me of buying this product from this business? Put another way "Why should I buy this product? And why should I buy it from you?"

So, from the very first seconds of reading any of your marketing literature, you need to be answering these questions and you need to do so in a way that grabs their attention. You do this by showing you understand their needs and concerns, how you can meet those needs and that you're going to do it "with knobs on".

It's crucially important to understand at the outset, therefore, that the language of powerful marketing is *benefits*. To do this effectively you need good preparation, on the front end… more on this later.

Features and benefits

You shouldn't have too much difficulty coming up with a list of relevant benefits for your products or services. The more you can come up with the better. What's more, there may well be many *features* of your products or services that could be expressed as benefits. Do not under estimate the significance of this; you could be missing a great opportunity to increase the power of your proposition.

Take, as a simple example, a hole-punch – here's how you might express some of its features as benefits:

Features	Benefits
Comes with plastic paper guide	*Accurate filing for all paper sizes*
Reservoir for punched paper	*No mess – punched paper easily disposed of*
Wooden base	*Attractive wood-finish base – will look great in any office*
Extra guide to avoid paper overload	*Clever device that ensures paper never jams!*

Get the idea? And that's just a simple hole-punch: just think of the scope for your offering.

If you wish to take full advantage of this approach, you need to start by setting out a table (like the one shown above) and just list absolutely all the facts and features you can think of relating to your products, services and even the way you do what you do. When you're sure you've covered just about everything, go through your list and convert each item into as many benefits as you can come up with. Remember, every benefit is one more good reason for your customers to buy from you!

Stay true

I've already said you must build the trust of your customers. Your marketing proposition is about catching their attention and convincing them of the benefits of dealing with you. However, real business growth is obtained through getting your customers to come back and buy from you time and time again. If you promise them things you know you can't deliver, believe me, they'll know too and they're unlikely to forgive you. Once you've lost their trust they won't come back.

Even if you're unimpressed with the moral argument for always being truthful, you must accept the very practical point that your marketing approach is only going to yield real fruit if you constantly demonstrate that you deliver on your promises.

If you feel there's a particular benefit that customers would really go for, but you don't provide it, the only effective way forward is to figure out how you can provide it and only then include it in your proposition. Don't even try to bend the truth, your customers will surely find you out – they're not stupid!

> ### Business sense...
>
> You'll have noted that throughout I refer to the need for acting consistently and with integrity, of seeking to build trust with your customers and indeed all your business contacts.
>
> I wish to make it absolutely clear that I'm not on some religious or moral mission here. I'm advocating this approach because it makes good business sense. It's very difficult to do business with people with whom you have no relationship. The stronger the relationship, the easier it is. A number of ingredients are required

for the building of any relationship but without trust it's difficult to see how any kind of real understanding between two human beings can exist.

I'd suggest that acting at all times with integrity is not just about maintaining a clear conscience, in the long run; it really is the savvy way.

Getting an edge

Any business that has some key advantage over its competitors will be able to use that edge profitably in some way – not surprisingly therefore virtually all businesses, whether the owners realise it or not, are constantly seeking this *competitive advantage*.

Apple Corporation's iPad was a spectacular example of a company with a product able to achieve such domination in a marketplace that it could generate literally billions of dollars in revenues. This is further underscored by the fact that those super-profits have since declined as the rate of innovation has slowed.

Such competitive advantage, in principle, can accrue at even the smallest level. Take, for instance, one restaurant in a large village. If you live in that village and want to eat out but don't wish to drive, where else can you go? Other restaurants in the area may be just as good but you can't walk there so the restaurant in your village has a competitive advantage on that point. It's probably not enough in itself to make the proprietor wealthy but it will, undoubtedly, contribute to his income.

In some way most businesses will have some form of advantage or advantages and it's important that you recognise, for your business, what these are and make sure that they are appropriately communicated to your potential customers.

We've already talked about differentiating your business in some way: this is, in effect, a technique for making the most of the uniqueness of your business and what it offers and translating this into distinctive benefits for your customers.

If you think about it, though, this is just making the very best of what's already there. If what you have is very good and wins you business, it's almost inevitable that someone else can copy it. Late Apple Inc. CEO, Steve Jobs, could also see this threat but on the basis that it's far more difficult to nail a moving target, he sought to maintain the iPad's position as market leader by constantly updating and upgrading the product... again and again. Consequently, Apple's competitors were, at that time, continually at least one step behind.

Of course there are many, many factors that work together that have created the phenomenal success of the Apple Inc. brand but there can be no doubt that the continued lead the company was able to maintain, right across its product range, was due largely to a constant flow of innovation that provided solutions its customers sought.

To achieve success in your business you don't need to match Apple's technique, nonetheless there's much to be learned from it. If you wish to enjoy the benefits of real competitive edge for your business, from here on you need to be looking at your business with the following key points in mind:

✓ *Understand what your customers are looking for now and what value they'd like to have in an ideal world.*

✓ *Consider how you might add value to your products and services – something that no one else does that takes you some way to achieving those ideal solutions.*

✓ *Make sure your clients or customers understand how your offering can meet their needs.*

✓ *When you've found something that works, start looking for the next thing.*

✓ *Keep tweaking and testing and tweaking and testing and constantly look to improve in some new way.*

These are the key underlying steps you need to follow in order to attain and maintain an edge that can bring huge benefits, in the long-term, to your business.

Never second-guess your customers

From personal experience I can tell you that it's frighteningly easy to fall into the trap of assuming you automatically know what your customers want. You don't. And even in those times when your results indicate you are in tune with your customers, this situation can quickly change; a new dynamic is introduced that can make your products or services completely obsolete.

A restaurateur knows best

Two partners in a local restaurant business, to whom my firm provided accountancy services, were offered a free business growth consultancy session to see if we could help kick-start their ailing business. Takings had gone through the floor so we started to look at ways of increasing customer interest. This was intended to be a standard brainstorming session with the aim of generating a list of techniques to start experimenting with.

By their own admission they had absolutely no idea what techniques they needed to employ to start moving things forward. On the other hand, without ever having made any reference to their customers, they were emphatically clear what wouldn't work... just about everything! Each new idea that was put forward brought forth the same stock response: "Oh no, that won't work".

"How do you know?" I would ask with growing frustration.

"Oh, it just won't", they responded, while exchanging confident glances.

> Admittedly intuition can be very powerful and should be listened to. However, it's not infallible, and if you've been acting in accordance with yours and it's manifestly not working, you need to try something new.
>
> We all need to accept that we don't automatically know what our customers really want – at best that's guesswork!

There are all sorts of reasons why people change their buying habits. It may be because some new invention creates a product that undermines the services you offer or even renders them irrelevant. This happened for manufacturers of cassette tapes when compact discs were first introduced to the market.

On the other hand such change may arise as a result of some new legal regulation, or how much money people have to spend and even just changes in social norms. For instance, who would ever have thought, 30 years ago, that the vast majority of the UK population would own their own mobile phones or would be able to write to each other, free of charge, without using letter-post?

These are all huge changes in the way people live their lives and, therefore, how they spend their money.

Getting to know your customers

Far too many small business owners commit insufficient resources to their marketing efforts – not surprisingly business growth is significantly inhibited. Those who do commit more resources often just wade in without any planning or indeed any consistent, coherent message that will tell prospective customers what benefits are on offer. Not surprisingly such activities, however earnest and well-meaning, produce disappointing results.

To compound the error, these disappointing results are often misinterpreted. I frequently get comments like: "Yeah, I once tried doing some marketing, it was rubbish – it was just a complete waste of time and money". That's a bit like saying "I tried to drive my car this morning but it had a flat tyre – cars are rubbish, I'm going to get rid of mine!"

If you want more bang for your buck, you need all your marketing efforts to be laser-focused on a powerful and consistent message that actually has some real significance and meaning for those you are aiming to influence – this means you need to get clarity on:

1. *Who you need to be communicating with.*
2. *How and where to find these people.*
3. *What their needs and concerns are.*

Then you need to develop a clear and comprehensive message to these people, using the right communication channels that demonstrate you understand them and their concerns. You also need to show how your offering provides a solution that is specific to their needs and – to put the icing on the cake – is, in some way, unique.

OK, I accept that's quite a lot to take on board and, so far, I've only told you what the direction your first foundational steps should be. So, now let's start to look at *how* you go about achieving all this...

Your quick-start research

Go into any decent bookshop or on the web and you'll find literally hundreds of books on how to market your business and with many of these texts, given time, you can truly transform your business – no doubt about it.

Among a plethora of highly effective techniques they'll show how to carry out your own original research to help you identify and locate those people most likely to be interested in your products and services and what techniques to use to most effectively get your marketing message across to them.

However, if you wish to kick-start your research by getting some real insights from those with experience in the same market niche you're planning to serve, here's an approach aimed at saving you time and helping you to get started on building good, strong communications as quickly and effortlessly as possible...

Finding your way

Here's where we look at defining who your customer really is and what he's looking for in terms of the product or service you provide. If you've been in business some time then you will have, at the very least, gone through the thought process of defining your customers and, given that you're currently selling to them, you may feel you can skip this section. *Be very careful here!*

You can get this roughly right and make sales but are you truly identifying who you should be talking to and what they essentially want? If you've not thoroughly covered these crucially important questions, then it's likely that much of your marketing efforts are wasted. The time available to you for your marketing is limited enough as it is, without frittering it away!

As a small business owner you're probably not going to have the resources to carry out elaborate, detailed market research and, for this reason, to some extent you have to accept that you must learn and develop your approach as you go along. So let's take a look at a simple, step-by-step approach; to begin with, from the perspective of a new-start business...

New-start business

OK, on the face of it, you're beginning from scratch here. However, as a start point you should, if you've taken any interest at all in the business you're about to embark upon, have a rough idea as to the profile of the customer you're going to be serving.

You should be pretty clear, for instance, whether you'll be dealing with the ultimate consumer or other businesses. You will also know, or should easily be able to identify, *other businesses that do what you do* – both locally and nationally. This is an incredibly important point because businesses that are already established, particularly those who are known to be successful, will have done most of their own research and testing and will know, from experience, what works and what doesn't.

"So what?" you may ask. Well, with a little research you can start to find out what techniques they use that work to their advantage. *If you think about it, it's impossible for them to keep it a secret* – these are systems for communication, on a grand scale, with the outside world! For instance, it doesn't take a highly skilled researcher to spot that one reason why major chain restaurants perform better than their smaller counterparts is that they employ a constant stream of innovative and effective promotions – one after the other – it never stops. This is really not difficult stuff to check up on.

If you're in the confectionery business, to give another example, why not check out what Hotel Chocolat are doing – just go into their stores, repeatedly, and check out the different types of promos they employ. I've done this myself, as part of my own research on behalf of a client. (I wish to confess, at this point, a weakness for those chocolate truffles... particularly the dark chocolate variety...)

More to the point, by watching who comes in and out you can see who their key customers are – if you're seeking to operate in the same market niche, you can pick up some seriously important (not to mention free) intelligence here.

If you're providing products or services to other businesses then investigate how and where your successful competitors communicate with their customers. Check out their website and, in particular, look for links. Google them and find out where else their name appears. From this you can usually tell to whom they are addressing their marketing messages – this, in turn, will help you to determine where you might start to direct your marketing efforts. Check out the social media sites: where are the established businesses directing their attention? Does advertising work for them? Check out various media – which do the successful operators use? Look for the patterns and how they work. Do they produce newsletters or a regular blog?

Investor research

It's also worth keeping in mind that large public companies operating in your market are the focus of attention of would-be investors.

"Value investors" for instance, will look closely at how the business is run in order to identify strengths and weaknesses and thereby determine whether the company's shares are a worthwhile investment.

Some companies are hugely researched and those carrying out that research often share the information they have with each other on public forums on the web. You don't need to participate but you can read what's been said and pick up on other people's research.

Information about such companies, some of it useful to you (though much of it not), trickles into the public domain largely thorough the national press or the web – but these enthusiasts, who carry out their own research, will pull much of this information into a more coherent whole, providing a source of knowledge that could be invaluable to you in your research.

Do not underestimate the importance of this approach – remember that when it comes to market research, someone out there will have done a huge amount of work in the markets in which you operate – you can save yourself an enormous amount of time, effort and heartache by gathering information that is already out there in the public domain.

Make notes as you go along and use them to gradually build a profile of your ideal customers; what they're looking for and how to communicate with them – but don't close your mind to the possibility of multiple ideal target customer groups giving you a choice of profiles to target with your own marketing activities.

As you carry out your initial research you should be seeking to, at the very least, answer a number of key questions...

Who are your customers?

To get yourself started in identifying who you are dealing with and what you need to be offering to them, you must begin to build a picture. The more clarity you have on the following points, the clearer that picture will be:

- ✓ *Age range/gender mix/geographic location*
- ✓ *Who will actually use your product or service? ... and just as important...*
- ✓ *Who makes the buying decision?*
- ✓ *How do you find them/communicate with them?*
- ✓ *What are they looking for (solutions, answers, needs)?*
- ✓ *What are their key concerns or challenges?*

What are your successful competitors doing?

- ✓ *Who are they communicating with?*
- ✓ *How are they communicating with them?*
- ✓ *What are their key marketing messages?*
- ✓ *What are the key benefits of their products or services and, in particular what, if any, unique benefits are offered? You may also find it useful to research up to five or six of your most respected*

competitors and try to identify patterns such as common benefits, etc. Can you employ these in your proposition or can you offer something even more attractive?

✓ *What promotional techniques do they consistently use? ie three for the price of two, free reports, free gifts, loyalty cards, etc. If these techniques are getting repeatedly used then it's likely they're being employed with some success – can they be successful for you?*

Pulling together what you learn

As you read these notes you may well come up with questions unique to you or your business. You may think of other issues you need to look at as you work through the research process too. If this happens, make a note immediately it occurs to you and add it to the suggested list of questions above.

You might also find it useful to set up a sheet of A4 paper for each of the above questions, using the question as your title and then aim to enter as much research information as you can to each sheet in order to provide as full an answer as possible.

Keep your notes brief but clear and gather everything new that you learn whether or not you can see the direct relevance to your business: what may seem irrelevant to you now may not seem so later when you have a clearer picture of your way forward!

Already operating your own business?

Don't worry I'm not going to throw a whole different set of techniques at you. In fact, all of the steps I've outlined for new-starts, above, apply equally to the established small business.

If you've been in business for some years, it's easy to fall into the trap of assuming there's not much other people can teach you – in my experience this is a dangerous notion.

We can all learn from others, no matter how much experience we have, and nothing stays the same for long. If you have competitors that have constantly, over an extended period, performed better than you, it's about time you started asking yourself why that is – the answer may well radically change your future!

The research I've outlined thus far is not difficult and won't take you eons of time to carry out. By taking this approach you'll be piggybacking thorough research carried out by those who have gone before.

It will not only assist you in identifying to whom you should be directing your marketing messages, it will also help you determine what buttons you need to be pressing, what value you need to be adding and what benefits you need to be providing.

Keep these particular points in mind as you carry out this process and build your notes accordingly. This will help you with your next, crucial, foundational step; that of building your overall marketing approach...

... But don't just be a copycat

The aim of this research is to give you important and crucial insights into what direction you need to be taking your marketing, the *where and how* of finding your customers and, therefore, quickly get some forward momentum.

To simply pick up what your competitors do and slavishly copy them could be disastrous as no two businesses are exactly the same. Just because it works for one of your main competitors, it doesn't automatically follow that it will work for your business.

Ultimately, the only real way to know what works for you is to try out the techniques you pick up along the way and carefully monitor the results. After you've tried something make sure you know how well (or how badly) your technique performed – then modify and try again... and again and work your way through it.

What's more, it is really, really important that as you proceed through your research you're constantly on the lookout for a different approach: something that no one else is doing. It could be a different angle or something that brings out the uniqueness of what you are offering to your customers.

Virgin, Richard Branson's group of companies, has successfully introduced a continuous stream of new ideas to established markets over many years. This has not just occurred as a result of luckily and spontaneously coming up with a number of random ideas that happen to work, rather it is the natural outcome of a carefully designed systematic approach for generating and developing new thoughts, inspirations and plans. Albeit on a smaller scale this approach can work for you too.

If you're doing nothing more than copying someone else, you're not bringing anything new to the party. Central to your marketing strategy, should be to differentiate your offering from everyone else out there. By all means take on board what you're learning as you go but you also need to constantly seek to add something that is uniquely you!

The end of the beginning...

Let's keep things in perspective here, there is no magical formula that you can put into practice from day one and make millions. Developing your marketing machine is an ongoing process which doesn't have an end but it must have the underlying aim of gradually getting more and more effective. This is achieved by an ongoing process of trying out new ideas, seeing how well they work, learning from the experience and moving forward from there.

Focusing on what has been learned from those who have *been there, done that* is a great way to quickly get some initial forward momentum but you need to be clear that when you've completed this important step, you've really only just begun.

As you complete this initial phase you should be starting to develop a clearer picture of just how you wish to position your business and its products and services with your target market – this will set the tone for all your marketing activities from this point.

In Chapter 5, we'll be looking at the next major step in developing your marketing arsenal: your powerful proposition.

Key points from this chapter

1. Your customers require your special attention. The success or failure of your business will hinge upon your ability to serve their needs and to effectively communicate to them that you're doing so. True, getting this right is not going to guarantee success but without it you'll fail.

2. Marketing should permeate your whole business. It's about matching the goods and services you provide with the needs of your customers. Given that serving your customers is fundamental to business success, it follows that marketing-related activities should figure in all your plans, actions and thinking.

3. Non-marketing activities are important too. Marketing is where you should focus your attention initially but you'll need financial, production and people resources to support whatever you're seeking to achieve. These will need to be taken into account before carrying through your marketing plans. Such resources will support or constrain your marketing efforts.

4. It doesn't matter how strong your marketing message is, if your product or service is poor quality you're never going to build strong customer loyalty. For the very best results you need to ensure that your offering serves the needs of your target customers... preferably "with knobs on".

5. Keep your eye on the ball. Make sure you're clear on your "four marketing aims" and the "savvy ground rules" and operate accordingly.

6. Get to know your customers. The most effective way to learn about your customers' needs is to patiently work with them and keep testing to find what works and what doesn't. This, of course, is a slow process – however, you can achieve some quick wins by following in the steps of other successful businesses. This approach can save you a massive amount of time and effort while giving you important insights into what solutions your customers seek.

CHAPTER FIVE

Your powerful proposition

IT'S CRUCIALLY important that in all your communications with your prospective customers you are transmitting a completely consistent message… every single time. If you're constantly giving out mixed messages and making contradictory statements you are, at best, undermining the strength of *all* your communications and at worst you're destroying your credibility. So it's really, really important that every time you communicate with your customers and your prospective customers, you do so with the same underlying, consistent message.

That's not to suggest that all your marketing communications should say exactly the same thing every time: certainly you can get the same underlying message across using different wording and emphasis. Nonetheless, your fundamental aim here should be to achieve a powerful consistency so that *all* your marketing communications *work together* to *constantly reinforce all the key points of your overarching marketing statement…* and each other.

In itself this is very strong reasoning for the creation of a potent, comprehensive and persuasive argument or *sales pitch* that will be your *powerful proposition*, but that's not all; there are more, equally compelling, reasons why you need to set out your proposition on the front end of all your marketing...

Why you need a proposition...

If you're not already convinced about the need for an underlying marketing message, just take a look at the following undeniable advantages of planning out your proposition:

- ✓ *Complete consistency in **all** your communications from day one.*

- ✓ ***All your communications will work together to reinforce each other** – how powerful is that!?!*

- ✓ *Each and every piece of **marketing literature can be put together more easily and quickly,** as all the groundwork has already been done – thus saving you time and money.*

- ✓ ***You'll be lighter on your feet** when you need to act quickly as new marketing opportunities arise.*

- ✓ *You'll have a **greater feeling of confidence** when preparing your marketing materials and this, in turn, **will save you time**.*

- ✓ *When you make any changes to your underlying proposition, **you can quickly and easily adjust** all your copy to your new template.*

- ✓ ***It makes you define, at the outset, what your products and services stand for** and how you will serve the markets in which you operate.*

- ✓ *Your proposition will, in itself, provide you with **a guide through your whole marketing approach** – in fact I heartily recommend that you use it in this way – see more on this in the next section.*

So before you can start churning out your highly effective marketing copy, you need to fully prepare that proposition.

What your proposition is…

In essence, your powerful proposition is a *comprehensive sales pitch providing a detailed set of compelling reasons why your customers should buy from you.* What's more, to give it all some serious oomph, each element of your pitch will need to be consistent with each and every other element – get the idea?

Life's a pitch...

Let's now take a look at how you can construct your detailed sales pitch, by considering what elements should be included in your proposition and how they might be set out for maximum impact.

As you work your way through these elements I'd suggest you start to make notes about how you're going to effectively match your products or services to what your target audience seeks. Don't rule out the possibility that you might need to make some fundamental changes to the content or quality of what you offer.

1. ***A strong opening***

   Start with an eye-catching headline – a real attention grabber!

   You could kick off, for instance, with a leading and relevant question – this is powerful because we all feel an impulse to answer a question and the presence of a question mark can draw the eye. You should be fairly short, sharp and to the point and aim at stimulating the reader to read on.

2. ***What it is and why you need it***

   This should connect with and directly follow on from your header.

   This is where you need to provide an impressive presentation of what your product or service actually does with all the benefits, laid out in order of importance, to your potential customers. Also, really important, if you wish to give your message some real bite, you'll need to crown it with some unique benefit.

3. Remove the barriers

This is where you must thoroughly address any concerns, worries or other potential barriers to customers buying from you. Never let it be said that empathy is not a powerful marketing tool!

What are the key barriers? Pose them all as questions you need to answer and then answer them. Remember this is not just about creating a great presentation; if the way you deliver your products or services creates one of those barriers, maybe you need to change the way you work!

4. Banish the perception of risk

One of the key concerns for any potential customer, particularly if they don't know you, is that you will let them down, in which case they will have wasted their money. The most effective way of removing this very real concern is to offer some form of guarantee. However, if your guarantee is to count it'll need to include the following key elements:

✓ *A specific statement that guarantees to achieve a certain minimum standard linked directly to the most crucial concerns of the customer. This may relate to a key function of a product or a crucial outcome of the service you provide.*

✓ *A clear penalty that you will pay if you fail. This has to be sufficient to reassure the potential customer – offering a free can of floor polish in the event you ruin your customers' expensive woodblock flooring isn't going to work! Make it worthwhile and significant. It could, for instance, take the form of product replacement or a commitment to rework any service in order to bring it to standard. Just make sure you **only** make guarantees for those issues over which you have full control – a bit of common sense and you can get the right result!*

✓ *Explain why you're doing it. This is important because a guarantee has to have credibility: you don't want your potential customers worrying that it's just too good to be true. So finish it off by answering the question: **Why would we do this?** Answer by explaining your experience and confidence that you will always achieve the standards you promise.*

5. Increase your credibility

Testimonials from delighted customers can be an extremely powerful source of independent confirmation that you actually do what you say you'll do. However, there are some ground rules...

✓ ***They need to be real*** *– By this I mean you should only quote what customers have actually said and, for real effect, you need to quote their name. If we're talking about the owner of a business, try and get permission to quote the business name too.*

✓ ***The testimonial needs to be specific.*** *No wishy-washy statements please: "Oh I thought their products were rather good..." simply won't do. For real punch, the quote needs to address, very specifically, customers' key concerns: "... whenever I ask for help I always get immediate action...* ***James Smith, ABC Engineering "**... Now that's more like it!*

✓ ***You need several testimonials****, each covering a different key aspect of your proposition – providing independent corroboration of the main benefits offered by your products and services.*

Obtaining great testimonials

On the face of it obtaining great quality testimonials from your happy customers might seem like a tall order. You may have seen such positive comments on web-sites and marketing literature and assumed that customers have just spontaneously written to the company because they were so amazed and delighted with the product they bought or the service they received, they just had to express their joy. This does happen, but not often.

The fact is, if you wish to obtain great testimonials from your happy customers you'll need to ask or apply a creative system which proactively invites feedback.

Here are some tips on how to obtain reviews you can use in your marketing copy:

- ✓ The best time to get **your great testimonial is immediately after delivery** – this is when the feeling of delight is at its strongest. So if you just delivered a great service why not ask for feedback right now?
- ✓ **Develop a system** so that you automatically ask for feedback after every sale.
- ✓ The **feedback form** is a really simple and potent way of doing this. Here are some important points regarding this approach:
  - ✓ If you make it quick and easy to complete, your response rate will be higher – scale of 1 to 10 ratings for a small number of different aspects of your products or services focuses attention and helps you to determine the areas in which you're exceeding or failing.
  - ✓ Not all feedback is positive – but this is good too as it gives you an insight into areas of weakness and what you may need to work on.
  - ✓ If you're scoring, on average, 9 out of 10, on some aspects, you could include this statistic in your marketing materials to support your message.
  - ✓ If you place, at the end of your form, a box asking for any comments about your products or services – you are inviting people to make positive comments. Better still, you could make your question more specific by asking for comments on a particular aspect of your customer's experience. You may also wish to change this question from time to time to provide you with testimonials that cover a range of strengths relating to your products of services.
- ✓ **Call your delighted customer** – this approach can also be systematised. Very soon after delivery of your great product or service why not call your customer? Once again you can use this call as an opportunity to get feedback so you can improve your service. If your customer speaks glowingly of their experience, at the end of the discussion you can ask them:

"would you recommend our product/service?" If they answer yes you can then ask if they'd be happy to provide a testimonial.

Again, you should try and make it as easy and convenient as possible. Note this also means you take control of what aspect of their experience you wish your testimonials to be focused on.

Strange as it sounds, you could offer to write the testimonials for them. This can be done by just paraphrasing what they say and then feeding it back to them; if they're happy with what you've written then you have a testimonial which is a genuine reflection of how your customer feels.

6. Action please!

It's crucially important that your potential customer is actively encouraged to take action – and to do it immediately. If they decide to leave it until later, a large proportion of people will not take action at all. You must have done this yourself: you defer and then let it drift and after a while you can't even recall why you thought it was a good idea in the first place.

Look for ways of stimulating action right now. You can do this in a positive way by offering something extra with a time limit on it, for instance. Your imagination is an important ingredient to add here.

7. Making it simple

Make it as easy as possible for your potential customers to take action. That means making it crystal clear what the next step is. It could be completing a coupon, emailing, phoning or clicking on a hyperlink… whatever… the more options you give, the better: we all work in different ways and so it's wise to cater for everyone. Don't forget to make it clear what happens once they've taken action; this removes any uncertainty and it makes it clear to the customer what to expect.

Fundamental to your marketing approach

One obvious question here is: How will my proposition fit in with my marketing strategy? The short answer is that your proposition should be the *centrepiece* of your strategy! In other words, I'm suggesting that you begin your whole marketing effort with your proposition and then proceed to build your marketing strategy around it. Can you see that you now have a basis for a completely consistent overall marketing approach?

The real strength here for you, as a small business owner, is that once you have your proposition in place you can get on with producing your marketing literature and then later go on to gradually flesh out the rest of your marketing strategy as you go.

From this point, when considering whether to apply a particular marketing technique, or indeed *how* to apply it, you should think about how it fits in with your marketing proposition. If there is a clash between the two, do not always assume that it's the proposition that should prevail: use this process to keep on refining your proposition.

Only fools rush in

When facing something a bit more challenging than we're used to, we all get that impulse to just get started, to feel that we're getting somewhere. For good or bad, when we do this, we are seeking to fulfil a desire to see some tangible progress as soon as possible – this is a perfectly normal and understandable human reaction but it's *not* automatically the smart move here.

When you feel that pull, no matter how strong, *you must resist.* Try instead to relax into your task of carefully setting out the solid foundations on which you will base all your marketing activities from this point onwards. Believe me, if you can do this it will pay you dividends, many times over, in the long run.

The research you've carried out, to this point, will provide you with a starting point for building a coherent, consistent message that will demonstrate, convince and persuade your customers that you can solve their problem, satisfy that need, quench that thirst or scratch that itch.

By constructing, on the front end, a comprehensive statement of all the benefits and value relating to the products and services you offer, you'll now find it much easier and quicker to compose all your marketing literature, in whatever form you wish, with the same compelling, consistent message.

Applying your powerful proposition

Your proposition will provide you with a comprehensive template from which all your marketing copy can be produced. From this template, for all practical purposes, you can now quickly and easily extract your copy and apply it in a variety of ways. This might include:

- ✓ *Your website homepage; providing summarised information regarding benefits.*
- ✓ *Your website details pages providing more comprehensive information.*
- ✓ *An all-embracing sales letter, which will include all the elements of your proposition. It's not always going to be appropriate to apply this in full but if you do, it can be incredibly powerful!*
- ✓ *Promotional letters, leaflets, brochures or even your very own app.*
- ✓ *Business cards/letterheads/compliment slips.*
- ✓ *Your blog.*
- ✓ *Your social media content – Facebook, Twitter, etc.*
- ✓ *Your elevator pitch.*
- ✓ *All forms of advertising.*
- ✓ *A basis for systems, selling techniques and sales pitch for your sales team.*

This list goes on, but you get the idea, right? Whatever method of promotion you're using, you need to be getting the same consistent message across every time.

OK, so what we're saying here is that, in order to effectively communicate with your prospective customers, you need to construct a single comprehensive message which you can then use *in whole or in part* for all your future marketing communications – that's what your underlying marketing proposition is all about.

Don't be too proud to get help

What you've learned about marketing thus far will provide you with a useful foundation on which to build. It is really important to emphasise that *this is just a starting point*; it's up to you to take it from here.

As you proceed you may encounter challenges that require specialist knowledge to guide you on your way – accept the principle that while you can do most of this stuff yourself, you can't always do it all.

There have been times where I've felt the need for input from an expert: someone who can introduce new ideas and a fresh perspective. By taking this approach you're tapping into irreplaceable knowledge and experience accumulated over many years.

Be ready to recognise when the time is right for you to do this and make full use of this highly valuable resource.

Key points from this chapter

1. Your proposition is a comprehensive sales pitch. It's a complete explanation of your product or service: what it is, what it does and what the key benefits are to the customer.

2. A strong proposition will have an eye-catching headline or title; state clearly what your offering is and does; offer some kind of guarantee and add credibility; if possible, with some positive testimonials from happy customers. What's more, it should also encourage the customer to take immediate action, while making it as simple as possible to do so.

3. Your proposition will serve you well. Setting out your proposition at the outset will give your message consistency, provide you with ready-made content for all your marketing messages and will form the hub of your marketing strategy. Last but not least, used correctly, your marketing proposition will save you lots of time!

CHAPTER SIX

Take control of your profits

GIVEN THAT profits are such a fundamental requirement for any business you'd think that absolutely all small business owners would understand how to operate profitably. Well, you'd be wrong; a frightening number don't even understand the basics about profit. What's more they have little idea of how much profit they're making as they go along and, if asked, probably couldn't tell how much profit they're making on their day-to-day sales.

To those of us who have never been self-employed, this might seem unbelievable, yet a huge number of businesses just muddle through, tending largely to do nothing more than work hard and hope for the best. Even those business owners who comprehend some of the basics can make some seriously bad moves that, at best, cause huge amounts of wasted time and money and, in some cases, lead to financial catastrophe.

Many of us have a mental block when it comes getting to grips with the money side of the business. It's almost like there's an unspoken belief that this stuff is beyond the understanding of most small business owners. Believe me *this is a complete myth!*

Rocket science it is not...

With just a reasonable understanding of simple arithmetic you can get your head around this stuff – no sweat! What's more, in this chapter, you'll see how to really get a grip on your profits and avoid making some of those seriously bad moves.

That's not all; with a better understanding of the how your business functions in money terms and at its most foundational level, you're going to have so much more confidence in dealing with the challenges you face and in the choices you make.

Keeping it nice and simple

You don't need to be concerned with any complicated principles or clever financial jargon. If you understand just a few underlying rules relating to how your business ticks in financial terms, you can then begin to truly take hold of your business and steer it in whatever direction you wish. I'm sure you'll agree it's much easier to understand anything complicated if you break it down into its key constituent parts and ignore the huge amounts of irrelevant information, which always cloud the issue. It just makes life easier to keep it simple.

Making the right moves

I want you to start taking action with confidence and in the sure knowledge that you *can* do this and that you know how and that's why I'm keeping it simple too – if you can understand the key underlying principles here then you're in a far stronger position, in the future, to meet the challenges you will inevitably face.

So, to kick things off, let's start by looking at some foundational rules about dealing with money in your business...

What's it all about?

When it comes to managing the money in your business there are just two things you need to focus on: *cash and profits.* Yep, that's it – take care of these two bad boys and you're completely in control.

Cash and profits are completely interdependent... joined at the hip... you can't have one without the other – get it? Think about this for a moment; if you're going to generate any profits, you need cash, and if you're going generate cash, you need to make profits. Let's look a little closer...

About cash

Cash, in this context, isn't just the loose change and the notes you're carrying around with you – we're talking about the physical cash your business has *plus* the money actually sitting in your business bank accounts. It's about how much lucre you can get in your sticky paws on right now, should you need it.

Cash is a consequence

You may have read newspaper reports of companies who allegedly failed because they ran out of cash. *Believe me, this never happens!* Running out of cash is always the effect... never the cause. This misleading media statement is a bit like saying that in 1066 King Harold died because his heart stopped. Sure his heart did stop but let's not forget he got an arrow in his eye first!

If your business runs out of cash it's because something, or more likely a combination of things, has gone wrong which caused that to happen. Your ultimate aim has to be to maximise the amount of cash available to your business and there are a broad range of activities that can contribute to how much you have at any time. It's up to you how you manage these activities – get it right and you'll have cash in abundance, get it wrong and, at best, operating your business will be a constant struggle.

We'll be dealing in some detail with many of these activities in Chapter 7, but now let's take a look at what should be your main source of cash: trading profit.

The anatomy of business profit

I'd now like to introduce you to some nice and simple underlying rules regarding sales and costs that will give you crucial insights into how you can maximise your profits. Listen up, guys and gals, these principles can make a very, very big difference to your financial decision making both now and in the long-term!

We're going to kick off by looking at the relationship between sales and net profit.

What is net profit?

This is a term you'll probably hear a lot and it's clear that many people feel confused about what net profit actually is. In fact it couldn't be simpler: to work out your *net profit*, all you need to do is *add up all your business sales* and *deduct all your business expenses*. Yep, that's it, nothing more than junior school arithmetic!

Of course, there can be quite a large number of different sales and expenses items to add up so, to make it easier to understand the detail, accountants tend to use a standardised format to work it out – which they refer to as a *profit & loss account*. Here's an overview of what that looks like:

PROFIT & LOSS ACCOUNT (Working out your net profit)

A: SALES	*The total you have charged your customers for the goods or services you've supplied*
B: COST OF SALES	*Any costs you incur as a <u>direct</u> result of producing, delivering or selling the goods or services referred to in **A**, eg materials, wages, bonuses, sales commissions, etc*
C: GROSS PROFIT (A - B)	*The profit generated from the sales you've made, or, sales (**A**) less direct expenses (**B**)*
D: OVERHEAD COSTS	*Includes all expenses not included in **B**, COST OF SALES, eg premises rent, rates, services, insurances, postage, printing, stationary, legal fees, office wages, etc*
NET PROFIT (C - D)	*This is profit after deducting all your expenses from total sales: **C** minus **D***

OK, now we've taken an overview of profit, let's take a look in a little more detail...

Two types of costs

As we've seen, your business net profit is the difference between the total value of the sales you make and the costs you incur and *some of your costs only arise when you make sales.*

These might include goods you buy for resale (eg shoes bought from a shoe wholesaler by a shoe shop), or materials you buy to make something you subsequently sell (eg the wood a carpenter buys to make furniture). Other examples might include wages you pay to people involved in the manufacturing process or even commissions to those who sell your goods on your behalf. Get the idea? These are all costs that only arise as a direct result of the sales you make. These are sometimes referred to as *direct costs* (because they are directly related to your sales) or *variable costs* (because they vary directly with your sales). OK so far?

These costs are very different in nature from, say, the rent you pay on your business premises or when you buy paper for your printer – such costs will have to be paid for whether or not you make any sales – these are normally referred to as *overhead costs* or *fixed costs* – they're fixed, they don't vary with sales. See the difference?

This fundamental distinction in nature between these two types of costs (variable costs and overhead costs) has *extremely important implications for you* and the decisions you make in the future – let me show you why...

Selling at a profit

The first challenge is to ensure that you make a profit on each sale you make. In other words, the price at which you sell your goods and services must be greater than what those goods and services cost you to produce, deliver and sell them.

OK, I accept it doesn't take a rocket scientist to work that out – it's so obvious it's hardly worth remarking upon – and yet, you'd be amazed how many small business owners start trading without even checking what direct costs they're incurring. Shocked? Yes, when I first discovered the abundance of this basic error, I was shocked too.

Let's be clear, if you can't get anyone to pay you more for the product or service you're selling, than what it cost you to produce it, you haven't got a business! There are situations where you're facing chronic business problems when it can be nonetheless worthwhile soldiering on for now... this *isn't* one of them!

A company that lost its way

A medium-sized international shipping company I was working for took over a huge company that was, at least on paper, more than four times its size. This newly acquired business was a top three operator in the shipping-agency business in the UK so, at the outset, this acquisition was considered to be a real *coup*. However, there was an obvious question: how could such an apparently large company be vulnerable to takeover?

Having been provided with trading results for the previous six years it was clear that the company, throughout that period, had suffered a steady decline in profits and over the last three years had been making significant losses. Along with a number of other senior accountants I was asked to look behind the figures to determine the factors that contributed to the decline of a company that had once been a major force in the industry.

One very interesting and enlightening development had been a decision taken, about five years earlier, to significantly drop their charges in order to stem the tide of declining market share. Many of the services affected by this decision were thus rendered loss making. That's right, it was actually costing the company more to produce the services it sold than the price it charged!

While it's not an approach I'd recommend, in certain circumstances this can attract customers that might not otherwise ever consider switching supplier. However, it's necessary to have a clear strategy for retaining that new business and to ensure that prices quickly revert back to profit-making levels. This is not what happened at all, though. In fact, many of these services *never* reverted back to profitable prices and, therefore, inevitably the company started haemorrhaging cash.

It seems almost inconceivable that a large organisation, apparently being run by a team of professional managers, would lose track so completely of how much profit it was making on its sales – but given this happened, the only way from there was down.

You can never afford to make this mistake – it's such a fundamental error but if the big players can take their eye off the ball, so can you – beware!

Making the smart moves

Covering your overheads

Not only do you need to be able to sell your products or services at a profit (referred to above as gross profit), the total gross profit you make on all your sales must be at least equal to the total of all your other costs (usually referred to as overhead costs or just plain overheads) in any period, in order to just break-even.

At *break-even* you're making neither a profit nor a loss – you're just covering your costs. Anything less and you make an overall loss, anything more and you're in profit, comprenez?

To illustrate the point, let's look at a very simple example:

Meet Jim Harris, he's about to launch his new company, *Widgets R Us Ltd*, which will manufacture and sell metal components called *Widgets* to the engineering industry. He needs to know what his likely profits will be for his first year. He's done some checking and found that he can expect to sell his Widgets for £20 each and the total cost of producing each one will be £15. In summary his gross profit for each unit looks like this:

	Per Widget
	£
Selling Price	20
Direct Cost	15
Gross Profit	**5**

He's also done his sums on overhead costs for his first year's trading and has concluded that they'll come to about £35,000. Here's a summary how these costs are made up:

Annual Overheads	£
Rent & Rates	10,000
Wages - Admin Staff	20,000
Other costs	5,000
Total Overhead Cost	**35,000**

Question: What do I need to sell to break-even?

One crucial question Jim has, right from the start, is: "How many Widgets do I need to sell in order to break-even?" This is really important because if it's far more than he can possibly sell, he has a serious problem.

Answer:

To break-even Jim will need to generate a total gross profit from all sales of £35,000 (which is equal to the total of his fixed costs).

Each Widget he sells generates £5 in gross profit – so we want to know how many £5s we need to equal £35,000; therefore the real question is: how many £5s are there in £35,000? The answer is: £35,000 divided by £5.00 = _7,000_ and here's what his profit statement looks like at this level of sales:

	£	£
Sales (7,000 Widgets @ £20)	140,000	
Direct Costs (7,000 Widgets @ £15)	105,000	
TOTAL GROSS PROFIT		35,000
Annual Overheads		
Rent & Rates	10,000	
Wages - Admin Staff	20,000	
Other	5,000	
		35,000
TOTAL PROFIT/(LOSS)		0

In other words Jim needs to sell 7,000 Widgets in order to generate a gross profit that will match his overheads – voilà, at this level of sales he has *break-even*!

The good news is that Jim's fairly confident he can make and sell significantly more than 7,000 units and therefore expects to make a profit in the coming year.

Can you see how significant this calculation is? If you don't use this approach *before you start trading* then you're running blind. I've seen many examples of people choosing an arbitrary sales and profit margin target, then they spend all year working to it only to find that, even though they've achieved it, they've still made a thumping loss!

In the Jim Harris example, by carrying out this calculation he knew immediately the minimum sales he needed to make to avoid a loss. If 7,000 Widgets is way beyond what he expects to sell in a year, his plans need a major rethink. OK, for him, this would be bad news but, as I'm sure you will agree, it's much better for him to find this out now, on the front end, than 12 months down the road when he's made a hefty loss and his bank balance is *in the toilet*!

How much profit do you want to make?

The above example provides a useful reasonableness test to determine whether your business has got any chance of turning a profit, but how do you determine how much profit you can make? Let's take another look at Jim's business...

Jim is pleased to learn he can make a profit but to really make his business worthwhile he needs at least a £25,000 profit – so...

Question 2: How many Widgets will I need to sell if I'm to achieve an annual profit of £25,000?

OK we're using the same gross profit numbers:

	Per Widget
	£
Selling Price	20
Direct Cost	15
Gross Profit per Widget	5

The overhead numbers are the same too but this time we've also added a target profit of £25,000 to the total so that now we're asking how many Widgets does Jim need to sell in order to generate £60,000 of gross profit?

	£
Overheads	
Rent & Rates	10,000
Wages - Admin Staff	20,000
Other	5,000
	35,000
Add Target Profit	25,000
Gross Profit Target	**60,000**

Right, if we now take his total gross profit target of £60,000 and divide it by £5 (gross profit per Widget) we get *12,000*. So now we're saying Jim has to sell 12,000 Widgets in order to achieve £25,000 profit. Let's see what Jim's profit statement looks like at this sales level:

	£	£
Sales (12,000 Widgets @ £20)	240,000	
Direct Costs (12,000 Widgets @ £15)	180,000	
		60,000
Annual Overheads		
Rent & Rates	10,000	
Wages - Admin Staff	20,000	
Other	5,000	
		35,000
Profit/(Loss)		25,000

From Jim's knowledge of the market he's serving he thinks that 12,000 units would be a tough target – but possible. He decides to be bold and go for target of 15,000 units for the year. Whatever happens from this point, by monitoring his sales and costs he will have a good idea, as he goes along, as to how much profit he's making.

If Jim now breaks down that annual target to 1,250 units per month he can monitor performance more closely – though he may need to make some allowance for seasonal sales variations and adjust his figures as new cost information arises.

Get the idea? By applying this approach you can create a very simple financial model, which will give you a broad idea of the financial return you can achieve at different levels of sales at an assumed price and based on likely costs.

But what if...?

The obvious next question, of course, is: what if Jim hadn't been able to make that level of sales or what would be the effect if he were to increase the price by £1.25 per Widget? Yes, it would be very useful if you could answer a range of questions like this in order to enable you to refine your targets and the way you work.

The good news is that you can do this and, in fact, it's quite easy. You can start by entering the above-mentioned format into a simple computer spreadsheet, using formulae to calculate profit margin per unit, total overheads and target profit margin. You can also use formula to calculate the number of units you'll need.

If you want to know, before you commence your business for your next year, just how much profit you can realistically expect to make, this simple approach is a must. Don't just blindly get started, hoping for the best, and then wait for your accountant to tell you, several months after the end of the year, how your business performed. An even worse sin is to wait for your bank manager to tell you when you've gone overdrawn.

Useful online resource

On my firm's website you can find calculators that will help with this – just go to **www.macrays.co.uk** and then go to **Resources/BusinessCentre/Business Calculators.** Here you'll find some very useful tools: *Breakeven Calculator, Gross Profit Calculator, How to make more profit calculator* and *Mark-up Gross Profit Converter* – why not give them a try?

So the order of play is...

OK, let's recap – First of all you have to be sure that you're making a gross profit on each item of product or service you sell. Then you need to be sure you can sell enough volume to first cover your fixed costs (at which point you're breaking even) and then reach a level that will give you the profits you seek.

Understanding these basic mechanics will hold you in good stead, not only in keeping a watchful eye on your profitability as you go along but also in aiding you with key decisions such as whether or not to launch your new business, or new product range or even such fundamental questions as to whether or not you should carry on trading!

If you're not in control of the key numbers in your business then you're just hoping for the best – and that's a very scary place to be when you've got a mortgage to pay!

How risky is your business profit?

When it comes to understanding the numbers in your business, you need to be clear on just how much risk attaches to the profits you earn.

If your fixed (or overhead) costs are very high relative to sales then you're much more at risk in a downturn than a business with relatively low costs. This is because even marginally small changes in sales can cause frighteningly violent swings in profit. Of course, this can be great news when sales are rising but when they're falling your handsome profits can suddenly turn into blood-curdling losses.

Let's look at a simple example:

Two companies, Highcost Ltd and Lowcost Ltd, operate in completely different industries but, as you can see below, in Year 1 they make exactly the same level of profit:

	Highcost Ltd	Lowcost Ltd
	£	£
Sales	1,000,000	100,000
Overheads Costs	950,000	50,000
Profit	50,000	50,000

Even though the bottom line is the same for both companies you can see that Highcost Ltd has a much higher level of fixed costs compared to sales than has Lowcost Ltd. Now let's look what happens when sales for both companies fall by just 10%:

	Highcost Ltd	Lowcost Ltd
	£	£
Sales	900,000	90,000
Overhead Costs	950,000	50,000
Profit/(Loss)	(50,000)	40,000

Wow, what a difference that 10% makes, eh? Lowcost is, of course, marginally worse off but Highcost has made a thumping loss!

You need to watch out for new business opportunities that have relatively high costs like Highcost Ltd. If you take on a business with this particular characteristic you're always going to have to manage that extra risk.

Don't get me wrong, I'm not suggesting you should always avoid such businesses but you do need to be aware of the risks you're taking on. I've often advised clients on the viability of businesses they are thinking of purchasing and rarely, in my experience, is this area of risk something they'd given any thought to.

Where I do identify such risk I don't automatically advise clients to walk away but I do make sure they're weighing up all the facts relevant to the decision they are about to make. I might, for instance, suggest that my client factors this risk into his price negotiations when buying the business in the first place.

Highcost Ltd is not unlike many manufacturing companies with large capital investment and heavy labour and financing costs. Service businesses tend to be less risky in this regard but that's not to say manufacturing businesses cannot make handsome profits.

If you're being offered a business that, year on year, achieves a profit that is low compared to overheads, you need to realise that it's not going to take much of a drop in sales to wipe that profit out!

When you're not sure about the risk

Sometimes, when you're considering a new plan of action, there are too many variables, too many unknowns to know for sure whether a particular new idea or approach is going to work – so if you're going to make any progress you'll need to test your idea in the real world and see what happens.

This, in itself, may sound like a high risk approach but if you carry out your experiment in a controlled and limited way you should be able to make your mistakes and learn your art in a manner that doesn't in any way threaten the future of your business when things don't quite work out.

Remember, when something you test doesn't work – that's not failure – it's just part of an ongoing learning process.

Trying your ideas out

When helping a successful medium-sized business to develop franchises across the UK, we didn't know for sure at the outset, whether or not it would be possible to create a business model that would work for each franchisee. So we tested certain key aspects of the franchise outside the geographical base of our client's business. We call this approach "piloting" and it's a common way of finding out how things work... compared to how we think things will work.

It would have been crazy to take a huge risk by assuming the whole thing would come together first time, spending hundreds of thousands of pounds, only to find you'd overlooked some fatal flaw in the business model. Better to test the theory on a relatively small scale and if the model works there, you can start to roll it out gradually on a larger scale. When you're checking the viability of a new idea or project in this way, you'll need to test how well the numbers work too.

Keeping track

The ideal way of ensuring you're keeping up to date on how much profit you're making is to produce a regular profit statement – sometimes referred to as "management figures". Done properly, this is set out in pretty much the same way that your accountant will produce your end of year accounts. By giving yourself this regular financial update you'll be in a better position to take timely remedial action should you need to.

Preparation of accurate management figures does require some level of accounting knowledge and that's why those businesses that can afford it will employ the services of their accountant to produce them. However, for many small business owners this approach is too costly. There is however a fairly simple, no-cost, approach you can take...

Your own profit statement

Why not produce your own quarterly profit statement? This is easier if you have some knowledge or experience, but if you follow the simple steps laid out below, you can get more of a grip on how your business is performing as you go along.

> **Getting a little help**
>
> Believe me, once you've set this up it shouldn't take you more than an hour each quarter to produce your profit statement. Initial setting up will take a little more time, but the steps below will show you what you need to do.
>
> If you're really not feeling comfortable about setting it up, why not ask your accountant for a little help? OK, the initial cost of your accountant's time might seem a large expense but this pales into insignificance

when compared to what you'd have to pay for them to complete your management figures on a regular basis.

Once you begin to appreciate the value of this process, you might also feel it a good idea to ask your accountant to check over your approach to make sure you're still on the right track.

Just keep in mind, the key aim here is to give you a rough idea of how your business is performing: precision is not necessary so don't waste time trying to achieve it.

The following approach is based upon the format referred to in the section earlier in this chapter: *Making the smart moves.*

Step 1: gross profit

As you go along you should be able to determine your gross profit with reasonable accuracy. Specifically, you should be clear on the gross profit you're making on each and every sale you make – if you're not doing this, how do you know you're making a profit at all?

I'd suggest that you maintain a running record (updated daily or at least weekly) for all your sales showing how much profit you're making and extract quarterly totals from this for determining your total sales, direct costs and (therefore) gross profit – for your profit statement.

Step 2: overhead costs – figures straight from your books

So long as you are keeping your books right up to date and entering all your supplier invoices as soon as you receive them you can, for the most part, pull the figures for your overhead costs straight from your books. You may need to make just a few adjustments though...

Step 3: adjust for annual or one-off payments

Let's say you pay annual insurance of £1,200 right at the start of each year. Your books will show that you paid out £1,200 in January but in the first three months of the year you only *incur* £300 – the rest would be evenly divided between April and December. This makes sense, right? If you're producing quarterly profit figures then to include all £1,200 in those first three months would distort your profit figure for that quarter so you need to spread it.

So you'll need to watch out for one-off payments like this and adjust accordingly. However, fortunately there aren't many overhead expenses where you're paying out in large lumps like this. Note, I used the word large: if any one-off or annual figure is not of significant value then you don't need to worry about making any adjustment.

Step 4: adjust for payments due but not yet in your books

You'll also need to watch out for costs you've incurred, at the end of your three months' period, that you haven't yet paid or haven't even received an invoice for – make sure you allow for these too.

Don't get bogged down with adjusting for piffling amounts – just focus those items that will make a big difference. Examples might include a delivery of stock received on the last day of the quarter for which you had not yet posted the invoice; also watch out for the tax and National Insurance not yet paid on employees' wages.

Keep in mind the Pareto Principle (or 80/20 Rule) – you will find that roughly 80% of the value of your overheads will be vested in about 20% of the items – so just concentrate your efforts on the larger value items only.

Step 5: working out your net profit

Just deduct your total overhead costs form your gross profit and, voilà, you have your net profit!

Laying it out

You could lay out your report in a computerised spreadsheet, using the same format adopted by your accountant when they provide you with your end-of-year profit & loss statement.

At first glance you might feel this way too complicated to take on – believe me it's really not that difficult! Once you've set this up and you have routines in place to ensure that your books are kept right up to date, preparing your report should fit easily into your end-of-quarter routine. Please believe me, getting a grip on the ongoing profitability of your business is not just something that it would be nice to have: it's a crucially important routine for putting you in control!

Pricing for profit

We've talked so far about the effects of sales relative to cost and how this can affect your bottom line profits, but, of course, how your products are priced is all part of the same equation.

This is an area so many small businesses struggle with and, in my experience, most get completely wrong. There are two very distinct camps when it comes to pricing: some business owners (minority) tend to be bold with their pricing and some prefer a more cautious line.

The pricing conundrum

Pricing high improves your profit performance for each sale you make and means that you'll need to sell fewer units of product or items of service to achieve your profit targets. However, there's always a limit to how high you can go with your pricing – beyond a certain point, your sales will start to decline as customers go elsewhere.

True, not all products automatically follow this rule, all the time. There was a period, for instance, when Rolls Royce could further stimulate demand for their cars by pushing up the prices. Those wealthy enough to afford such luxurious cars were looking for exclusivity and by raising the price Rolls Royce were attaching a more elite label to their products. However, this situation rarely happens and in our fast-changing world, even when it does, it seldom lasts long.

Ultimately, there's only so far you can go with raising your prices – beyond that point sales volumes will inevitably fall and then so will profit. Equally there's only so far you can go with the ultra-cautious approach of continually cutting your prices in order to try and stimulate demand – after all you can't go lower than the cost of producing what you're selling and the *thinner* your profit margins, the more product you have to sell just to break-even.

If you want to maximise your bottom line profit and retain customer loyalty, then, in truth, you're seeking that price at which:

✓ *Customers will buy because they believe they're getting sufficient value to make it worth the price you're asking and…*

✓ *Where you, as the supplier, are not giving away too much value.*

In my experience, most small business owners tend to assume that the price customers are willing to pay is lower than is in fact the case.

When the numbers don't add up

In the firm of accountants of which I am a partner, we don't go out of our way to pick up bookkeeping work; it's low-margin and fairly labour-intensive work. However, some clients need us to do their bookkeeping as well as deal with their annual accounts and tax.

Our proposition to clients is high quality with plenty of added value while being competitively priced. With our bookkeeping service however we keep our prices particularly keen. So you can imagine our surprise when one of our clients told us he was moving to another local practitioner who was offering to carry out the same service at half the price we were charging.

We knew immediately that the accountant (a sole practitioner) to whom our client was defecting was making a fundamental error in the way she was operating. From experience, it was clear that at the level of prices she was quoting she would have to work very, very hard to make a reasonable living. There certainly wouldn't be enough profit in the work she was taking on to enable her to employ someone to help with it – so she was going to have to deal personally with everything for her clients, as well as for her own business.

If you're well organised and efficient in the way you work you may be able to cope... for a time... but eventually the sheer volume of work involved will overwhelm you and once you get behind (say through holiday or illness), it's murder trying to catch up.

Just three months later, with his VAT return more than five weeks overdue and no real prospect of it being done by his new accountant, our exasperated ex-client came back to us – in the circumstances it was no big surprise.

Of course most small business owners will, in their approach, fall somewhere between the two extremes of high and low pricing but in the end the approach taken will be based largely on guesswork and intuition, but it doesn't have to be this way!

Smarter pricing

It is particularly interesting to note that underlying the above approaches is a common willingness to second guess what the customer will pay. For me this amounts to little more than flapping around in the dark. If you want to know how much your customers will pay, why not ask them? Yep, that's right – if you truly wish to find the answer to this crucially important question why not just *get it* "straight from the horse's mouth"?

Don't worry, I'm not going to ask you to stand on the High Street with a clipboard trying to catch the attention of passersby with a set of annoying questions. More effective than this is to continually *test* your prices. Employed correctly, this is not a one-off exercise in determining customer response to the occasional price increase: this is about setting in motion an ongoing process of testing your pricing on all your products or services and learning from your customers' responses.

What if?

I once worked with a client whose prices were far too cautious – sure, his sales volumes were very strong, because he was undercutting all his local competitors. The only problem was that his profit margins were so wafer thin his sales volumes, though high, still weren't high enough for him to achieve any more than subsistence-level profits.

On top of that, he was working all hours and continually chasing his tail in order to deal with the high volumes he was processing – not a particularly satisfactory situation I'm sure you'll agree.

As we started to explore how we might improve his approach to pricing it was immediately apparent this was a subject that caused him some discomfort. I could sympathise with this: it's easy to fall into the trap of assuming that any tinkering with your prices is likely to be detrimental to your profits in some way.

"OK," I asked, "to what extent would your sales fall if you increased all your prices by just 1%?" After careful reflection he decided it probably would have virtually no effect – in fact he rather doubted anyone would notice. "So why don't you raise all your prices by 1% today?" I asked. He beamed at me as he affirmed that he'd do exactly that.

"OK," I counselled, "but when you do this, you need to carefully monitor the response you get." He now needed, on an ongoing basis, to start testing and monitoring his pricing – after all, if a one percentage point price increase was not a problem, how do you know that 2% or even 10% is a non-starter?

P-E-R-L-E-A-S-E don't tell me you just know!!

As we have already covered, this principle of experimenting with something new and then monitoring the response you get is absolutely fundamental to the ongoing growth process. It's rarely a great idea to assume you know how people will respond – just test the idea and let them tell you. Carefully monitor the response you get and then modify and refine accordingly... and then repeat... and repeat. Get the idea?

It's not just about price

Have you ever bought a particular product or service and thought: *That's great, but wouldn't it be even better if it gave you this or did that?* It happens all the time. The so obvious next question is: where can you go to find that gadget that will do that extra clever thing or that service where you get extra help with that one area that has always been a concern for you?

The great irony here is that, more than likely, there'll be someone out there who does that, naturally, as part of the service they provide but, guess what, they simply don't mention it in their marketing or advertising. How crazy is that? If you knew they did that thing, you and many other eager customers would beat a path to their door and buy from that supplier time after time.

If, as a customer, you want to know the price of a product or service, all you need to do is look at the label... but determining all the benefits that go with that price is like some big secret!

Are you guilty of this? Do you communicate *all* the relevant benefits of your products and services? Because if you don't – and you need to listen up here because this is a really, really important point – *all your customers or prospective customers have to go on is the price.* Believe me, most of us are looking for great value, but if we're not told about all the value that comes with a product, then all we've got to go on as a point of comparison is the asking price. Not surprisingly therefore, if that is all we've got to go on – yes you've guessed it – *we go for the cheapest.*

This is a lose/lose situation. The customer loses out because they have no way of finding the value they seek and as business owner you lose out because you're competing for customers purely on the basis of price and therefore giving value away! Take my word for it, *competing purely on price alone is a mug's game.*

What about value?

The principle here is that you need to clearly communicate *all* the benefits of buying from and dealing with your business and you should be continually looking to add new benefits so as to differentiate your offering from that of your competitors.

So, in effect, you're removing that direct comparison on price. How can you be compared on price if your product and service range is so varied from everyone else? Simple answer: you can't!

> **Key Point:**
>
> Your customers will pay a fair price for good value – where that value is fulfilling a particular need or solving a problem they have. *When you can effectively communicate that value, price becomes a secondary issue.*

The savvy way

The savvy business owner knows that the more value you add, the higher the price you can charge and that, very often, this extra value costs you nothing – in fact, you may already be doing it, but just failing to let your prospective buyers know it.

They also see price as just one element of an overarching marketing approach and realise that, while some customers are looking for the cheapest deal, most people are looking for *value for money* (not the same thing at all!) and where they perceive there's more value, which is relevant to their needs, they will gladly pay a premium for it – no doubt about it.

A last word on pricing

What is the true price of the product or service you're aiming to sell? The answer, of course, is the amount customers are prepared to pay for it. My maxim here is: let your customers tell you what that price is. Testing your prices will tell you what works and what doesn't. It's a principle that's easy enough to understand but will require a good deal of time and effort to apply. If you truly want to find that price that's going to sell your wares in sufficient volumes to achieve the profits you seek, surely it's worth that effort.

Beware the fear of failing…

Is every price you test going to work well for you? Of course not, with anything you try in business you'll have your misfires – how else do you expect to learn? The savvy business owner knows that, very often, the only sure way to find out what works is by determining what doesn't.

So don't be fearful of getting it wrong – if you always avoid trying new ideas through a fear of failure you'll severely restrict your ability to grow your business. In my experience this is one of the main obstacles to growth for small business owners.

Key points from this chapter

1. Take full control of the financials of your business by focusing on cash and profits. Remember: these rely heavily upon each other.

2. Your current cash balance is a consequence of how well you manage a broad variety of activities but those activities related to generating trading profit are of key importance.

3. Make sure you're achieving a worthwhile level of profit on each sale you make: otherwise what's the point?

4. You need to know, before you launch a new business, or each new product range, or begin each new trading year, how much profit you can expect to make and what level of sales you need, to achieve those profits. If you're just hoping for the best you're playing a dangerous game!

5. Keep track of your profits as you go along. Simple management figures are easy to produce and will keep you in control.

6. Getting your pricing right is crucially important for maximising your profit. Don't assume you know the best price – let your customers tell you.

7. Avoid trying to compete purely on price. Add value to your offering and effectively communicate all the benefits. Add colour, avoid boring shades of grey!

CHAPTER SEVEN

Cash when you need it

Cash-profit is king

PROFIT, AS referred to in the previous chapter, is the difference between the total value of what you sell your products or services for, and *all* the expenses your business incurs in, generating those sales.

It's crucially important to note, however, that this sales figure takes no account of whether you've been paid by your customers.

There's a crucially important point to grasp here...

> *Even great profits are not much good to you*
> *unless you can convert them into cash!*

You've only made a *cash-profit* when you've actually been paid for the sales you've made. So, when it comes right down to it, managing your business finances is really about *maximising the cash available to your business...* the main source of which is cash-profits.

Maximising your cash

It's vitally important to appreciate that a broad range of factors can affect just how much cash is available to your business at any point in time. Your actions or omissions will determine to what extent these factors will work in your favour – no doubt about it; *it's up to you to take control.*

Becoming cash clever

If cash is the lifeblood of your business, then it stands to reason you need to keep your finger on the pulse (sorry about that.... couldn't resist) and you can only do this effectively by proactively managing the following key issues:

- ✓ *The trading profitability of your business.*
- ✓ *Your effectiveness in converting your profitable sales into hard cash.*
- ✓ *Maintaining a healthy balance between the amount of cash your business generates and what you, the business owner(s), take out.*
- ✓ *Planning for all the significant payments you need to make like the purchase of a major item of equipment or paying your taxes.*
- ✓ *Managing creditors (the amount of money you owe to your suppliers).*
- ✓ *Managing stock (such as raw materials you've not yet used or items for sale you've not yet sold).*
- ✓ *Planning for all your short-, medium- and long-term cash-flow needs so you always have the funds you need, when you need them.*

Having considered the topic of profitability in Chapter 6, this chapter is dedicated to providing you with key tools and techniques for taking control of each of the other items in the above list. Let's start by making sure you've got a watchful eye on what's happening in your business right now...

Getting a grip

Fundamental to good knowledge of what's going on in your business is a reliable and accurate set of financial records That means accurate, up to date accounts that reflect how much money you've got in the bank, how much you owe and how much you are owed. You also need to know how much you've sold and spent (plus what you spent your money on!).

All businesses have to keep records – this is a fundamental requirement. For starters HM Revenue and Customs expect all businesses to maintain adequate records so that business profits can be accurately calculated and easily checked, should they decide to carry out an enquiry.

However, if you're going to get a grip on the finances of your business, the quality of your records will need to be far higher than this minimum standard.

Believe me your needs are far more important than those of the any government agency. Even some accountants are guilty of missing the point here: the primary aim of your record keeping should be to provide you with information of sufficient quality to give you a clear picture, on an ongoing basis, of what's going on in your business and *every other consideration is secondary.*

This is not just about monitoring your profits: as a minimum, as you go along, you need to know:

✓ *What your current cash position is. Don't assume your bank statement balance will tell you this: the cheques you've raised in the last two weeks may not all reflect here nor will any standing orders or direct debits due to hit your bank account tomorrow.*

✓ *How much profit margin you're making on your sales.*

✓ *Based on that margin, whether or not you're selling enough to cover your monthly overheads – if you're not, you're making a loss and this means you need to take action… now!*

✓ Whether you're getting paid by your debtors quickly enough and who your slow payers are. Some small business owners are so lax on this that they forget to chase debts for months, thus increasing the chances of not getting paid at all – crazy as it seems, this really happens!

✓ How much cash you can safely draw out of the business without causing serious cash-flow problems. Believe me failure to address this point is so widespread it has become one of the most common reasons for business failure!

✓ How much you've spent and what you've spent it on.

If your record keeping approach provides you with this information then you'll be much more in charge of your business than many of your fellow small business owners.

Getting it sorted

For sheer convenience and economy of your time I'd suggest you can't beat a reliable bookkeeping software package. These days there are plenty of low-cost packages around and the better ones come with comprehensive assistance on how to operate them.

You don't need any financial expertise to get going with this and if you ever get stuck, a five-minute chat with your accountant will sort you out. Remember it's in your accountant's interests that you get it right – after all it's going to make their life so much easier when they're preparing your accounts at the end of the year.

Properly used, these bookkeeping packages will give you much greater insight into the current state of play with your business and crucially this puts you in control. Sure, manual bookkeeping systems can still provide you with adequate records for your VAT return and to enable your accountant to produce your end-of-year accounts, but they won't conveniently fulfil all the crucial information requirements that will give you control of your business.

This "helicopter view" of your financial position is crucially important for your business and for your peace of mind. The only real information gap with a standard bookkeeping package relates to up to date measurement of profitability – please refer to Chapter 6 to ensure that you have this covered.

Getting paid – taking control

If I had to name one thing that my clients complain of most, it's the problem of getting their customers to pay up. No doubt about it, huge amounts of both time and money are spent, often wasted, in the process of converting those hard-earned sales into hard cash.

On one level it's easy to sympathise because, when it comes to paying up, some of your debtors can be a real pain. I can't help feeling though that many small business owners make life unnecessarily difficult for themselves by not organising their admin properly and, quite frankly, operating on a hope and prayer.

There are some businesses, because of the nature of the industry in which they operate, which don't need to provide credit to their customers at all. If this is true for you, then great. However, if you do, like so many other businesses, need to offer credit terms on the sales you make you'll need to accept that the process of getting paid needs to be very carefully managed if you're going to save yourself a lot of heartache!

Of course there's nothing you can do to 100% protect your business from problem debtors, but there are a number of key steps you can take to significantly reduce your risk. Let's take a look at some of these...

Be careful who you deal with

Among many small business owners there's a dangerous misconception that all sales are good sales. Clearly it would be downright foolish to sell a product for less than it cost you. Equally, it would be crazy to give financial credit to someone who is unlikely to pay you or at best will make you wait many months for payment.

Whenever you deal with people like this you can potentially lose on a number of levels...

✓ *You may never get paid so all your related time and money is down the drain.*

✓ *You get paid... eventually... but you spend many months chasing up with telephone calls, statements, letters, etc, which all increases your related costs – so a large part of your profits goes down the drain.*

✓ *Because the money you're owed is in your debtor's bank account rather than yours – there's all the bank interest you've lost!*

✓ *The time you've wasted could have been spent on other more profitable business or even on growing your business.*

✓ *The money you've wasted or even lost is never recovered and its absence from your bank account could put the survival of your business in jeopardy – particularly if the sums involved are relatively large.*

OK, now let's take a look at ways you can get better protection from losing out in this way...

Think through the credit you allow

All too often small business owners unthinkingly allow credit that causes cash-flow problems even where debtors adhere to agreed credit terms. This over-generosity is to some extent understandably borne out of an over-eagerness to get the business at all cost – but sometimes that cost can be too high!

Consider, for example, the owner of a building contractor business who agrees to construct a large extension for a customer but asks for no deposit and no stage payments as the project progresses (this really happens!). This project could take weeks or even months to complete (for reasons outside his control) and in the meantime he's paying out for labour and materials and probably has to pay interest on an overdraft or loan to finance all this. Don't underestimate the finance cost here – on one project alone it could be very significant – but over many projects the costs can be crippling.

If you're incurring costs well ahead of ultimately getting paid by your customer, you need to look for ways of coming to an arrangement where you're not sticking your neck out too far. Seek out ways of offering benefits to customers who will make advance payments or pay more quickly – in the long run it will save you enormously in finance costs and it may save you a huge amount of time that might otherwise be wasted in chasing debts.

When it comes to carrot and stick, in my experience, the carrot is far more effective, so seek out ways of positively inducing your customers to act in accordance with your terms of business, rather than by coercion. That way you win and they win and, just as important, by avoiding sanction you're maintaining stronger customer relationships for the future.

Get an independent credit check

There are a number of well-known credit agencies that can help you determine whether or not someone you're about to deal with is likely to be a serious credit risk. Armed with this information you can then make a judgment as to whether you wish to deal with them.

If you get a report showing that a particular potential customer is a serial bad debtor then you should act accordingly. You're better off concentrating your efforts on good customers. Someone who has a reputation for not paying can never really be considered a good customer! That said, where you've been advised that extending credit is risky, there's nothing to stop you offering to sell on a cash-only basis – but if you get a negative response to this it's probably best to simply walk away.

> ### Take care with credit scores
>
> Be careful not to blindly accept credit scores of major agencies – they can, as I've learnt from experience, be misleading. Clients of ours who we know to be solid, reliable payers have been allotted ratings that unfairly suggest otherwise. You'll therefore need to be discerning about the information you're given.

Learn from your experiences

In our own accountancy practice we've dealt with clients who, while they haven't necessarily come to us with a poor credit rating, in practice have really messed us about.

These are people who fail to provide the information needed to complete their returns – often missing statutory deadlines (sometimes by years!) and then will suddenly wake up and want everything brought up to date... yesterday. So now you find you've suddenly gone from a situation where you haven't been able to get hold of them for months and months, to one where they're impatiently calling you every day to check how you're getting on with this "urgent" matter.

Then, when everything is finalised and you seek payment of your fees – suddenly, guess what, you can't get hold of them again!

Of course we've all had to deal with people who are this unreasonable, but isn't it just a little bit foolish to keeping dealing with them time and time again? If you've got any customers like this, take my advice and ditch them!

Never risk too much on any one customer

We've had clients who have allowed individual key customers to accumulate upwards of £50,000 in credit. This is a very dangerous road to take. Usually, of course, they pay up but you only need one debt of this magnitude to turn bad and suddenly your business can be in real trouble.

I'd suggest you carefully set credit limits for each and every customer and *make sure you enforce them* – as soon as you start to relax your rules on this one, you're on a slippery slope.

Yes, I know that in some industries applying such rules can be difficult and you may even encounter industry norms that work against you on this. Nonetheless if you wish to protect your business from the dangers of financial over-exposure you must address this issue!

Dealing with the big players

In recent years I've heard many complaints that some larger businesses – often well-known and apparently *respected* in their industry – have imposed unfair and unreasonably harsh terms on those small businesses with whom they work.

This might take the form of requiring as much as 120 days' credit or pre-setting the prices they'll pay at such a level that the small business is left with a pitifully small profit margin. In some cases, lamentably, these two techniques are applied in combination. If this isn't bad enough, these large organisations sometimes further abuse their power over the small business owner by taking even longer to pay than the agreed terms.

Big contracts with these organisations may seem, at least on the face of it, highly attractive, but in some cases when you get into the detail you begin to realise just how punitive they are.

One key point often overlooked by small business owners is the cost of the credit they're allowing here. If profit margins are thin to start with, the inherent interest charges can easily turn that small profit into a loss.

As a small business owner you don't have the power to change the behaviour of the large organisations you work with – but you do have the power to walk away.

Don't be seduced by the large contract that keeps your employees busy. Wages paid for work done on unprofitable business is no good to you – the numbers really do need to add up here. You have been warned!

Getting your act together

Getting paid by your customer can be significantly delayed if you haven't got keen procedures in place. We've come across instances where business owners are taking upwards of 30 days after supply of products or services before they even raise an invoice to the customer – can you believe this?

I've even come across examples where the supplier has left invoicing so long, he completely forgot to invoice thousands of pounds in sales and it was only a couple of years down the road, when a new bookkeeper was appointed that they realised what had happened – this is madness!!

You should hardly need me to point out that the sooner you bill your customer the quicker you'll get paid – even the most prompt payers are unlikely to chase you for an invoice. If this is an area of weakness in your business I'd council you *deal with it right now*.

Proactively getting paid

This is another area where many businesses are extremely lax – for some people it's almost like once they've raised an invoice they then just hope for the best! *Payment of your invoices is not something that just happens: it's a process and you need to proactively manage it.*

Why you need to manage your debtors...

1. *The longer you leave an unpaid invoice the less likely it is you'll ever get paid! It's fairly obvious that if you haven't chased up payment of an invoice six months after you raised it, it's going to be much, much tougher to collect than it would be if you'd been contacting your customer, on a regular basis, from day one. However, just one week can make a difference too; one of our clients was the very last person to get paid (and it was a five-figure sum) before the company he was dealing with went into liquidation – if he'd left it just a few more days he would have been among a long list of creditors who lost out.*

2. *It's worth keeping in mind that every single day money is owed to you, sitting in someone else's bank account, it represents interest lost!*

3. *Once an unpaid sales invoice exceeds your credit terms, not only do you need to be taking action, you need to be seen to be taking action. If you fail to act – surprise, surprise – some of your debtors will spot this and use it against you!*

Action points for you…

To rise above these problems you need to employ a systematic way of working that keeps you in control. It doesn't need to be highly sophisticated nor does it necessarily have to take up a great deal of your resources – in fact, operated correctly, a structured approach will save you pots of time. You'd need to tailor your approach to the way you prefer to work – but as a minimum your debt collection system should include the following elements:

1. **Check it out**
   Before you even allow credit, make sure (in so far as you can) that you're not dealing with someone who is a bad credit risk. Credit agencies can help in this regard. However, do not for one minute assume that a person with an apparently unblemished credit record means zero risk – nothing in business is so black-and-white. That said this procedure will at least weed out the obvious high-risk debtors.

   Even if a prospective customer comes up with a poor credit rating you could still deal with them on a cash-sale basis – so look for ways of making your sale this way. It might be worth pointing out to your customer that they could still get up to 30 days free credit on their credit card if they were to pay you this way.

2. **Your little red book**
   Maintain records of your experience with all your customers so that if they mess you about next time around you act accordingly. On the other hand, if you have, for some reason, restricted credit to someone in the past but they have since proven themselves more reliable, you might consider gradually improving the credit terms you offer.

3. **Make your position clear**
   Set clear credit limits and stick to them. Circumstances will determine what these are but when setting them you should be keeping the above points in mind.

Clearly state your credit terms on your invoice: "30 days nett" is the popular refrain.

4. Bill them quickly!

Set up an easy-to-operate and speedy system for generating invoices immediately a product is dispatched, service completed or project stage reached. None of this "I'll get round to it later" malarkey! Get it billed straight away and you're more likely to consistently achieve this if the billing process is nice and simple.

5. Keep your eye on the ball

Regularly review sums due from customers. Small businesses have access to relatively inexpensive software accounting packages from which you can run up-to-the-minute reports that will tell you how much you are owed, who owes it to you and how old any particular invoice is. From this helicopter view you can quickly tell where you need to concentrate your efforts, particularly if you're wishing to focus your attention on large and old debts.

You can also run reports that highlight when any of your customers have in some way exceeded their credit terms. By running regular reports that identify problem debtors you can guard against accidentally allowing more credit – which might make a bad situation much worse. See more on this below: Keeping your debtors in check.

6. Keep communicating

Send out statements every month. This ensures that those who owe you money are regularly reminded of the fact. Also, should your invoice get lost in the post, the debtor in question can't argue that they were blissfully unaware of the fact you sent them one!

7. No sitting on your thumbs!

Take care to ensure that you have in place automatic procedures to identify sums due that are outside predetermined credit limits and take prompt action once a debt gets older than your terms.

Keeping your debtors in check

Here's an approach that will help you collect overdue invoices and keep your financial exposure to a minimum...

Put the brakes on further credit

If a debt is overdue you have a problem. At an early stage you may not consider it to be serious problem and if it's a relatively small amount it may not be a critical one – but it's still a problem. Of course it could become a bigger problem if you were to allow more credit to the same customer – and that's why, as soon as you realise that a particular customer is not sticking to your credit terms you need to consider putting a stop on any further credit – at least until the current outstanding debt is cleared.

I'm using the word "consider" here, because circumstances can vary widely and you're going to need to apply your judgment in each case in order to determine whether or not it is appropriate to take what is, after all, quite a significant step and one that could adversely affect your relationship with your customer. So it's not a decision to be taken lightly.

On the other hand, if this debtor is someone you've never dealt with before and they're not taking your calls, chances are getting paid is going to be at best hard work and it would therefore be foolish to expose your business to more risk here.

This is a sensible precaution that may have the additional advantage of getting your debtor's attention. If he calls you to query the action you've taken, all to the good – you now have an ideal opportunity to discuss the debt that's overdue.

Accept it's *us against them*

Recognise you're now in competition with your debtor's other creditors. Think about it: if your poor-paying customer is still in business they must be paying some of their creditors; they're simply not paying you! So, if you just meekly (or apathetically) do nothing to collect your debt, you're going to be well down the pecking order and if they're having cash-flow problems you could be waiting forever!

It therefore follows that you need to compete to get paid and the harsh reality is that the more you communicate (badger even), the more likely and the more quickly you'll get paid.

Just put yourself in the shoes of a business owner who is struggling with cash-flow problems. Some of your creditors are hounding you and making your life a complete misery while others seem content to let you pay in your own good time. Who are you going to pay first? Not rocket science is it? An unfair way to work, I know, but there's no point in ignoring reality just because it offends your sensibilities.

Some bad debtors may not be that bad…

If your debtor has a cash-flow problem but is upfront and offering to pay on a reasonable, scheduled basis then you should be prepared to negotiate. Clearly it's not in your interests that their business fails: by doing this you're improving the chances his business will survive and therefore you're more likely to get paid and even get more sales in the future.

The fact that they're being proactive in this way is a positive sign in itself and giving support when a fellow business owner is struggling may well mark the beginning of a long and mutually fruitful working relationship.

> Most likely your difficult debtor will be paying *some* of their creditors this month; you need to work towards improving your chances of being one of them. So the next question is: what steps can you take to apply this pressure on those who are being uncooperative and evasive?

Cranking up the pressure:

1. **Reminder letter #1** – I'd suggest this is dispatched within one week of the credit limit being exceeded. This allows sufficient time for cheques posted within a couple of days of the agreed credit period to have arrived. This letter needs to be polite but firm. Something along the lines of:

   Dear xxx,

   I am writing to you to point out that our invoice 123456 is now overdue. Can you please take action to make settlement as soon as possible.

   I thank you for giving this your kind attention and look forward to your prompt response.

   Yours sincerely…

   [You might also wish to attach a copy of the statement of accounts for good measure!]

2. **The follow-up call** – After allowing a reasonable period for this letter to arrive, you could now follow it up with a phone call asking when you can expect payment. Once again you should be polite and firm and always try to obtain a commitment to payment by a certain date.

   Of course, debtors may be difficult to contact and if they do prove elusive after a further (say) 30 days you should move on to…

3. **Reminder letter #2** – I'd suggest this is a much firmer letter which points out that payment is now seriously overdue and should be settled without further delay:

Dear xxx,

I am writing to point out that our invoice 123456 is now seriously overdue – I would therefore request immediate payment.

As clearly indicated on our invoice, our credit terms are strictly xx days nett. Further credit on your account has already been suspended and future credit is unlikely to be provided where our normal credit terms are not adhered to.

I therefore look forward to your prompt remittance.

Yours sincerely…

4. **Follow-up phone call… again** – *Whatever you do, don't hide behind your letters – just because you're sending formal and tough warning letters, it doesn't mean you now don't need to try calling by phone. Your efforts are much more likely to succeed if you use correspondence and telephone calls in combination. Even if the debtor doesn't take the call, usually they'll know you've tried to call them and this all adds to the pressure you're exerting to get paid.*

   If, 30 days after sending your second letter, you've still not been paid and you've not managed to speak with your late payer then it's time for…

5. **Reminder letter #3** – *I'd suggest you make this your final letter communication regarding this matter, and it should be laced with a threat…*

Dear xxx,

Despite previous reminders it would appear that you have still failed to make payment in respect of our invoice 123456.

I must therefore inform you that unless we receive full settlement of this invoice within 14 days of the date of this letter we will take appropriate action to recover this debt, without further notice.

I would also point out that, in accordance with our normal terms and conditions, interest will be charged on all outstanding sums that remain due beyond our stated credit terms, in addition to any costs incurred in collecting this outstanding debt.

Yours sincerely…

You'll note, in my suggested letter, I've not specified exactly what action I plan to take if the debt is not paid; there are three key reasons for this.

✓ *There are a number of ways you can go from here (I'll explain what they are below) and by not stipulating your plans you're keeping your options open.*

✓ *When you've got to this stage, your debtor has now really messed you about so you don't owe them anything – I prefer to get them guessing (if they care at all). Anyway, I don't advocate you defer taking your next step too long – so they'll find out soon enough.*

✓ *I can't help feeling a threat of action, without being specific about what you're planning to do, can sound more ominous. However, you may disagree and if you're clear on what steps you now wish to take, you can be specific.*

Be prepared to carry out your threats

One particularly psychologically important point to keep in mind is that if you make a threat you really, really need to be prepared to carry it out – and do so in the time frame you've declared. If you fail to do so, your debtors will spot this and your credibility is shot – and like I said before: they will use it against you... mercilessly!

6. Following it all up with hard action

OK, you've sent out regular statements, withdrawn further credit, issued three reminder letters and followed up with phone calls. You should find that your system has yielded payment from most of those tardy payers. For those who have still failed to make payment, or respond at all, you'll now need to consider your next step, so let's look at your main options:

a) Solicitor's letter

In essence this letter is a bit like Reminder letter #3 (see above) except it's on your lawyer's letterhead. Some debtors might be influenced to pay up in response, though the feedback I've had from clients over the years indicates that results have been mixed, at best.

It's also worth keeping in mind that if it doesn't work there's rarely any further recourse than to take the debtor to court. For most small debts this will be the small claims section of the County Court and you could have done this yourself anyway, without the expense of your lawyer's intervention.

That said you could well find this approach works well for you. The only way to find out for sure is to give it a try!

b) Court action

Ultimately, making a claim for payment through the courts may be your only way forward but it's worth being aware that even if you're successful in court you may still have difficulty in enforcing the judgment. That said I can tell you we and many of our clients have used this approach in the past with some success.

c) **Direct action**

If the sum is of sufficiently significant value you might consider visiting that debtor's premises to demand payment but do keep in mind that such an approach would not be appropriate where the debtor is genuinely disputing your invoice. This is undoubtedly a confrontational course of action and not something that everyone would feel comfortable with. However, it can be an effective way to step up pressure when all other attempts at communication have failed.

d) **No-win, no-fee agents**

One alternative approach I favour is the no-win, no-fee, debt collection agency. In my experience they can be a very effective way of getting payment. OK you may have to accept you will lose some of the money due to you as you'll have the agent's fees to pay but in many cases it's worth the time and anguish it saves you.

It's worth noting also that these agencies are usually effective at what they do – and if they fail to get your debt paid for you, well, it hasn't cost you anything! In my experience (admittedly, this is purely anecdotal) this is a very effective way to proceed. In some cases, if it has to go to court, you'll find the agents will represent you. Although this may mean extra expense for you, it will, once again, save you the hassle!

Another plus is that some of these agencies will even agree to try to apply their costs to the amount claimed from the debtor, so it can finish up costing you nothing!

Getting the right balance

The implied assumption in the above guidelines is that the debtor is being deliberately awkward and evasive – and perhaps never intended to pay anyway. However, as we all know, it's not always that clear-cut and lots of late payers will present to you circumstances where greater leniency, flexibility and understanding is required – once again it comes down to your judgment as to how and when to apply the full force of the techniques and tools now available to you.

Do these techniques work every time? No, of course not – life's never that simple. However, on average and over time your cash-flow will be in much better shape if you take control in this way.

Another powerful advantage here is that you can save yourself a huge amount of time and hassle – it may not seem that way as you start to put these systems in place but, believe me, the wasted time and money that can result from poor management of the debt collection process can be immense.

Used appropriately, these tools will help you minimise the total amount of money you're owed by your customers at any point in time, and this all contributes to a stronger ongoing cash position for your business.

Managing the cash you've got

No matter how effective your systems are for bringing in the cash, if you don't properly manage the cash you've got you can still run into serious difficulties. Cash management is one area where we find small business owners make some very serious errors. Let's take a closer look...

Balancing earnings and drawings

I should hardly need to point out that to continually spend more than you earn is simply not sustainable – it's pretty obvious really, hardly worth mentioning, right? So why is it that governments, right across Europe and beyond, have completely ignored this basic truth – for decades? Yep, that's right, year in year out, they've all spent more than they've generated in (tax) revenues and they've borrowed the difference. And they're all paying huge amounts of interest on those debts.

Where do they get the funds to cover all this interest and to pay for all the other things they've committed to do? Yes, you've guessed it, they borrow more money! When described in this way it may seem unbelievable – nonetheless this is what has been happening and, as I write, it's happening now!

If governments can make such a fundamental error, it is perhaps more forgivable that small business owners do it too – but there's no escaping the financial realities here – that it will end in business failure is absolutely inevitable; it's just a matter of when.

Horror stories

We've seen instances of businesses borrowing funds from the bank, which masked the fact that the business owners were drawing funds out for personal use at a level much higher than the income generated by the business. Only when the loan funds finally dried up did they realise they'd been living beyond their means.

This is a trap that's very easy to fall into, particularly if you're not keeping adequate records. If you're not keeping a careful eye on this, how can you possibly be aware that in the next couple of weeks you'll need to have funds available to pay a large sum to a key supplier? If you draw those funds out and spend them now you've got one major problem! There are all sorts of reasons why the funds currently sitting in your business bank account are not a reliable reflection of your profitability – *you have been warned*!

How much can you safely draw out of your business?

Intuitively you might think, so long as you're drawing out less then you're making in profits (after tax) you're OK. In the long-term this is generally true but watch out, in the short-term, for large lumps of expenditure that don't necessarily get counted in the profit calculation.

A good example would be an expensive piece of equipment you paid cash for. This could cost your business tens of thousands of pounds but only a small proportion of this cost might be reflected in your profit calculation in any one year (as depreciation). On the other hand, your bank balance will reflect the full value immediately.

"I work hard, therefore I deserve a good salary"

This is a response we often hear from clients when we've pointed out they've drawn too much money from their business compared to business earnings. To be honest, I completely sympathise with this sentiment, but if the earnings aren't there it's simply foolhardy to draw cash out – ultimately the business will run out of sufficient cash to pay the bills – eventually suppliers will stop supplying and when that happens, the business has no means of trading; kaput! Governments might be able to ignore this simple rule, at least for now, but *you* can't!

Plan for major purchases

Perhaps you have to replace a couple of vans or maybe you need some new computer equipment: whatever it is, you're going to need funds to make that purchase.

For so long we've been tempted with (apparently) mouth-watering loans from the many high-profile lenders offering easy access and easy terms. Don't be fooled though: borrowing money is going to cost you and this will therefore make your new acquisition much more expensive. One simple and far less costly way of making sure you have the funds you need, when you need them, is to plan well ahead and start saving now...

Making provisions

Let's say you've just bought a new van for your business. You hadn't planned for this expenditure so, as you didn't have the funds available, you had to borrow the money.

Now you have your new van you're going to be paying off the loan, with interest and in three years' time, when you need your next new van, you start again. You may be even quite pleased with yourself because you found a really great low-interest deal – but, of course, that's never as good as *no* interest at all.

If you'd thought it through, chances are you'd have realised much earlier that you'd need to fund this van and could have saved up at least part, if not all, of the money you needed. So now you have your brand new van which you know you'll have to trade in, in about three years' time – what are you going to do next? Are you going to continue with the current expensive loans treadmill? Or will break out from the current pattern of behaviour and start building the funds that will put you more in control of your business?

Consider the advantages of saving in advance rather than borrowing:

✓ *With the funds available you can act quickly should a great deal arise.*

✓ *If you can pay cash you're in a stronger position to get a discount.*

✓ *You'll be earning interest on your savings as you go along, so you gain financially.*

✓ *You won't be paying interest on a new loan so, once more, you gain.*

✓ *You reduce your risk by reducing your commitment to regular loan repayments.*

The arguments for saving rather than borrowing before you make any major purchase are very powerful and yet the most common approach of small business owners is to do nothing until those additional funds are needed and then borrow expensively.

When I've suggested this approach in the past, some clients have protested they can't afford to put the money to one side each month – and yet, bizarrely, they have no problem with committing to expensive monthly loan payments. This is a kind of short-termism: we see money sitting in our bank accounts and think we're better off than we are – so we spend the money that we're going to need at some point in the future. If you can easily identify your future spending needs now, and gradually build up your funds you can make those cap-in-hand loan applications a thing of the past!

Don't get me wrong, I'm not saying you should never borrow funds; there are definitely situations where taking out a loan is the smart move to make, but to borrow habitually and in the unfocused way described here, is absolutely not one of them.

Lumpy payments

You can even apply this approach to major payments such as large annual insurance premiums, your annual tax bill or even your quarterly VAT return payments. Building up funds now, on the front end, has got to be a much better approach than waiting for the payment to come due and then scurrying around to pull the necessary funds together to pay it.

A common refrain I hear in response to this is: "Yes, well it's not quite that easy when you simply don't have the funds to do it". Sorry guys, this just doesn't wash – of course you have the funds, when the payment comes due, you *must* pay it – or your business will fail. You can avoid having to scrape around for the money each month if you act *now* – put the money to one side *now* – all I'm suggesting is that you get realistic about what your financial commitments are… before they come along and bite you!

Managing creditors

We've looked at dealing with people who owe you money, now it's time to put the boot on the other foot and consider how you manage the level of credit you receive from the various suppliers of goods and services to your business.

Of course, it makes sense for any business to make full use of the credit offered by its suppliers. If someone is prepared to allow you time to pay, this is a bona-fide part of the terms and conditions of doing business and *you should make full use of it.*

The balancing act

Whether or not you give credit to your customers or receive credit from your suppliers will depend in part on the businesses you're working with and norms for the industry in which you operate. You would not, for instance, normally expect credit for the purchases you make of your daily newspaper or the bottle of milk you buy from your local supermarket.

However, if you're in a business where you need to offer credit in order to compete then you have to obtain the funds to cover this. If, for example, the total value of your debtors, at the end of each month, remains constantly at around £40,000, this means that you're continually out of pocket by this amount. Sure, many of your debtors may well have paid you by the end of the month but by that time, new debtors may well have taken their place to approximately the same value.

If your business is extending large amounts of credit at any particular point in time, you need to bridge the gap in your finances somehow and one significant source can be trade credit. Thus, a key aim for you should be to obtain as much of this credit as possible – because this is just about the only significant source of finance you can get which is *absolutely free* – and this is what makes it so important!

Gold dust

Obtaining trade credit is an extremely crucial issue for your business – free credit is like gold dust.

Just think about it; if you don't have the cash to make an important payment then you may have to take out a loan and pay interest on it. Even if you do have the cash to make that payment you're taking money out of your bank account (which you should, at the very least be holding on deposit) so you're losing out on the interest you would have earned.

In view of all this it really is worthwhile taking steps to maximise the availability of trade credit available to your business in terms of both how much you can obtain from each of your suppliers and for how long.

Credit really is a part of the deal

When you're purchasing resources for your business you need to take into account a broad range of issues: price; value for money; product quality; reliability and suitability. These are all crucially important considerations but factors relating to the supplier need to be taken into account too. For instance, can they be relied upon? How long will it take from initial order to delivery? Will they come through in an emergency, what guarantees do they offer and, of course, *what about trade credit?*

The absence of free credit, in effect, increases the cost of the product or service you're buying – it is therefore vitally important that you factor credit terms into the choices you make.

Negotiating for credit

You can improve the deal you get by proactively negotiating with your suppliers and, particularly once you have proven yourself as a loyal customer and reliable payer, renegotiating the credit terms you're getting.

There's an old but very true saying: "if you don't ask, you don't get". While you don't always get what you ask for, if you persist, in the long run you'll benefit from taking the initiative with your suppliers in this way.

Demonstrate you can be relied upon

Once you've managed to negotiate credit terms with your key suppliers you really must keep to your part of the bargain. This gradually builds your credibility as a trustworthy debtor by demonstrating *you can be relied upon to do what you say you will do.* This has two positive effects: it strengthens your suppliers' confidence in you thus reducing the likelihood of credit terms being withdrawn and, just to add icing on the cake, it puts you in a much stronger position to press for even better credit terms at some point in the future.

Reliable debtors are the best sort for any business to deal with so the more you demonstrate your reliability in all your dealings with your suppliers, the better the position you are in to obtain an improved deal on *all* your terms and conditions.

Keeping a clean record

You should pay close attention to your rating with the recognised credit rating agencies – a poor rating can significantly reduce your access to new credit. If, for any reason, your business has a weak rating you need to take action to tidy it up and seek advice on how it can be improved. Often, just a few simple steps are all that is required to get your easy access to trade credit back on track.

These days you can check your credit rating easily and cheaply online and depending upon the type of business you're in it may be worth doing so on a regular basis. As discussed earlier in this chapter, credit ratings can be misleading but they are nonetheless often referred to by your would-be suppliers of credit and therefore cannot be ignored.

Keep your stocks (inventories) under control

Frightening amounts of your hard-earned cash can get tied up in stocks that sit on the shelves too long before being sold. And the really worrying point here is that the longer stocks sit there the more likely they will become completely obsolete.

This represents losses on two levels: on the one hand you're losing out because funds tied up in stock could otherwise have been held on deposit earning you interest and there's the far more significant expense associated with writing off the total cost (to you) of that stock.

Large retail organisations like Marks and Spencer spend huge sums remunerating skilled buyers and investing in sophisticated stock-control systems in order to minimise their losses from stock obsolescence – they truly understand just how expensive it can be if you get it wrong. So what steps can *you* take to reduce your risk here? Let's take a look…

Stay focused

I cannot honestly say I'm a DIY enthusiast but occasionally I'll need to repair something in the home that needs that special little washer that will just do the trick. In the past I'd call into one of those superstores and be told that I'd need to buy the whole unit, for which I'd have to pay up to 20 times what that washer would have cost! I'd then go to the little DIY corner shop, just down the road, and hey presto the owner, who'd probably been running his shop for more than 30 years, would know exactly what I need and he'll sell it to me for a few pence.

We've all got stories similar to this and we revel in the savings we made while lamenting the disappearance of those little corner shops. Of course that transaction was of real benefit to me but of absolutely no value whatsoever to that small business owner. He probably had thousands of pounds of small items of stock just like that washer, some of which would probably sit in his shop for years – taking up valuable shelf space and tying up his cash.

On an emotional (and perhaps somewhat selfish) level I want such businesses that try to provide that helpful support service to all-comers to succeed, but I know from experience that running your business in this way is really not smart. You have to get a balance here – you simply cannot be all things to all people.

We've come across restaurants with huge menu choices offered to their customers. To support this they need to buy in a much broader range of perishable stock. You only have to visit any of the more successful restaurant chains to see that they focus on what they know, from experience, their customers are most likely to purchase and from a relatively small menu range they will constantly tinker and test to find the most popular dishes.

It's really important that you carefully manage the range of products and services you offer – be clear on who it is you're serving, what it is their looking for and what else they're most likely to buy at the same time. Oh, and don't forget: *all* items in your range of products and services need to carry a profit margin that's worth your while!

Don't reorder too early

Many retailers I've worked with have an almost pathological fear of running out of stock and for this reason tend to hold large stocks of their main lines. As soon as those stocks go out on the shelves, more stock is ordered. If you think about it, there's kind of cycle of events taking place here: you order your stock, you take delivery, you pay for it, you sell it and finally (hopefully) you get paid for it.

During the time between paying for your stock and getting paid by your customer, cash is missing from your bank account. This, of course, costs you interest – either in terms of what you pay for a loan or what you lose by not having your spare funds on deposit.

So the shorter you can make that period between purchase and sale the better, right? Better still if you could reverse them so that you were able to sell the product before you paid for it. Pioneering retailers who built those successful supermarket brands we've all come to know did exactly this. They would buy stock on credit and before the due date for payment they would have sold it from their market stalls and taken delivery of the next consignment. Now that's smart business! It may or may not be possible for you to be quite that slick but you need to ensure that as soon as possible, following receipt of goods from your supplier, you're selling those goods and getting paid for them.

Getting a better balance

On the one hand you don't want to tie too much cash up in stock, on the other you don't want to run out of stock either – a bit of a conundrum that! However, achieving the right balance doesn't have to be about guesswork and gut-feel judgments; there are ways you can take control here. Let's take a look at some tried and trusted techniques already out there and being used successfully by small businesses just like yours...

1. ***You need to know what you need to know***

    There's no getting around having access to good, reliable, up to date data regarding how much stock you're holding at any point in time. If you don't know what your stock levels are right now, what earthly chance do you have of taking control?
    Answer: none!

    How you keep tabs on your stock will largely be determined by the nature of the business you're in and the resources you have available to you. However, they don't always have to be costly; you will generally find there's a trade-off here between cost in terms of money on the one hand and time on the other.

    These days, retailers where stocks are constantly being depleted can access rather clever till systems that, linked to a computer, can monitor stock levels and automatically warn you when you need to reorder. Some may consider these till (or point of sale) systems rather expensive, but it might be wise to compare this cost with what you lose by constantly over-stocking (and the wastage that goes with it) or running out of stock and losing sales.

However, clever till systems are by no means the only way of monitoring your stock levels. For instance, a multinational company I once worked with would arrange boxes of stationery in stacks, with a piece of paper part way down the stack which had the following statement clearly marked on it: **"When you reach me you need to reorder!"** *Simple but effective, eh?*

What issues do you have with managing your stocks?
How can you apply this simplistic, no-cost approach?

2. Great supplier service is key

Wouldn't it be great if you could wait until you've sold the very last item of a particular product line and then within just a few seconds of having made a telephone call to your supplier, in they walk and stack your new stock straight on the shelves? In the real world, of course, this is mostly impossible. From the time when you place your order to the point when the product is delivered can be days or even weeks.

The next best thing, of course, is to know exactly where you are with your supplier: can you rely on them to deliver when they say they will? Can you get them to commit specifically to a delivery lead-time that will help you to minimise the volume of stocks you need to hold? As we have already seen, there are a number of important criteria you need to consider when deciding which suppliers to use – and this is definitely one of them.

3. More than one basket for your eggs

If you sell a number of key lines that are critical to your business, you need to take steps to insure against your supplier letting you down. The most effective way of doing this is by using a range of suppliers: that way, if one supplier fails you, you have someone else you can turn to.

Just sticking with one supplier because (say) they're cheaper than everyone else is short-sighted at best and a dangerous path to take. I'd suggest, if you can, you rotate your patronage between at least three regular suppliers of key stock items you need – though you may need to modify this number according to circumstances and the industry in which you operate. This keeps a variety of relationships ongoing and helps to maintain loyalty across a broader (and therefore safer) supplier-base. When you do this you're increasing the chances that, should your stock shortages reach crisis level, one of your regular suppliers will be able to help you out in your hour of need. I'd also suggest you constantly remain on the lookout for alternative suppliers whose product range and way of working better suits your needs.

Whichever way you go, take the time to build strong relationships with your suppliers; a reliable supplier of key products or services is, after all, of fundamental importance to your business.

You can always make it better

Like so many other aspects of your business, you can benefit from constantly seeking to refine and improve your current approach – whatever your current approach happens to be! Learn from the mistakes you will inevitably make and develop your own unique system of working.

Key points from this chapter

1. You can't spend profits; that's why it's so vitally important for you to have an efficient process for converting all your profitable sales into cash as quickly as possible.

2. If you allow credit to your customers you must carefully manage the process of getting paid. The initial work involved in setting this up may seem like it's more effort than it's worth – this is an illusion! In the long run this will save you a massive amount of time, money and anguish.

3. The profits-to-cash conversion process is just one element of what should be your overarching aim of maximising your cash reserves. Other key elements that you'll need to manage include: profitability; balancing what you draw out of the business with sensible provision for future expenditure; trade credit and stock.

CHAPTER EIGHT

Getting the funds you need

To borrow or not to borrow: debt is the question

BORROWING MONEY can help you through a short-term cash shortage or get that piece of equipment you urgently need. There'll also be times when a striking business opportunity lands on your plate and you need funds right now before that window of opportunity closes – if you're going to wait for sufficient funds to accumulate then, in all likelihood, that chance will be missed, never to return.

No doubt about it, there are clearly times when borrowing funds is the right – and sometimes the only – way to achieve your goals, but is it always a good idea to borrow whenever you need to make a purchase?

As demonstrated in the previous chapter, under *Plan for major purchases*, for predictable, large purchases the smart move is to build up your funds in advance so you don't have to borrow. Now, though, let's take a closer look at the main pros and cons of borrowing for your business…

How about a little OPiuM?

You may have heard financial experts extolling the virtues of growing your business with **O**ther **P**eople's **M**oney. The principle here is that it's worth borrowing money if you're confident that by investing it you can earn substantially more than the price you're paying in interest and charges. It's a strong argument and many people – savvy business owners included – have successfully built their businesses using this approach to finance.

Of course, if the project for which you use these funds were to fail or seriously underperform then you might find that the cost of funds turns out to be greater than the return on your investments, causing you to incur significant losses.

In the final analysis you'll need to make a judgment call based upon thorough research and planning. If you're serious about growing your business you'll need to accept some level of risk but this can be minimised by doing your background work thoroughly.

Taking a carefully considered, calculated risk is not the same as sticking your neck out and taking a gamble – if you do this then you're just hoping for the best and that's no way to run a business! Using *OPiuM* to grow your business has its place – but before you commit, always make sure you've weighed up the risks as well as the return.

A loan you want for the funds you need

It's impossible to predict, with 100% accuracy, what's going to happen tomorrow let alone next month or next year and that's why you always need to be prepared for the unexpected. In Chapter 11 we'll be looking at the defences you can put in place to avoid disaster but it is worth making the point here that a cash-buffer is by far the best defence against unexpectedly running out of funds.

In the absence of these buffer-funds you'll need some other form of temporary funding facility in place to tide you over should you suddenly find that your business is chronically short of cash. There's also the situation where, in the normal course of trading, your cash balance fluctuates sharply. Let's look at your options here...

Emergency cash

If you're managing your cash effectively then the chances of running into cash-flow difficulties are significantly diminished – but you can never, ever 100% guarantee to avoid the occasional short-term disaster and, working on the *Plan B* principle, it's wise to have in place a financial safety net.

So, unless you have a substantial sum on deposit that acts as your financial *cushion*, I'd suggest you consider having a bank overdraft facility in place. I would emphasise that your aim should be to *minimise* how much you use it. Nonetheless, it's reassuring to know it's there should you need it.

The aim of this facility is to provide a buffer; nothing more, nothing less. If you routinely make full use of this facility, then you no longer have a buffer. Before you know it you've come to rely upon this relatively expensive loan and the next tempting step is to increase the facility in order to restore that buffer. Don't go there! I should hardly need to tell you that this won't work and in fact will only lead to increasing your debts and the onerous interest charges that go with it.

The smart move is to set up an overdraft facility for the odd occasion when you might need it, at a sensible level that will be sufficient for your needs, should a need arise and then proceed to do your very best to ensure that you never use it!

Coping with the ebb and flow

For some types of business the funds available from day to day can be a bit unpredictable; one day there's plenty of cash in the bank and the next the business is in danger of going seriously overdrawn. This is a common challenge and is relatively easy to resolve.

For those occasions when you can find yourself temporarily short of funds a bank overdraft facility, once again, is usually the best solution. This is a really effective way of covering those unexpected and unavoidable shortfalls in cash. Sure, interest rates on this type of loan do appear relatively high but you should weigh this against the fact that you only pay interest on the funds you draw – no more, no less. It's very flexible because it's like a tap you can switch on and off, as you need it.

Another subtle, but crucially important, advantage is that an overdraft facility is designed to match your cash-flow needs. Let's say you receive a major order from one of your key customers. This is great news: you need the business they're giving you and you want to get future business from this source too… so you're looking to hit the ground running. To this end you'll need to invest in materials and labour a while before you present your invoice and ultimately get paid.

Of course you could take out a "term loan". This is a loan of a fixed sum of money for a fixed period of time. "Fixed" is the operative word here: it's not very flexible. Don't get me wrong, loans of this nature do have their place but where the need is less predictable, or for a shorter period, the overdraft facility is a much better fit.

This is because an overdraft provides you with a credit line which is there if you need it, when you need it and costs you nothing if you don't make of use of it. Sure, you'll need to pay a nominal sum to set up the facility but this is small potatoes compared to the cost of failing to match your needs to the correct type of finance.

However, like all things in life you need to maintain a balance – clearly it's not smart to rely on just one single credit line from one single source – banks are well known for withdrawing overdraft facilities at short notice and for those too reliant on them, the very survival of the business can be threatened when this happens.

Some people may tell you that banks would not be so brutal as to put a small business in that position... hmmm.

Getting perspective

Having the safety net of a bank overdraft facility is never a bad idea, particularly in the short-term but, as already mentioned, I'd strongly suggest you consider trying to wean your business off it in the long-term. If you want to avoid being constantly tied in to your bank, why not start to build up a buffer-fund that sits there in readiness to be called upon as and when you need it.

Those funds will sit there earning you interest and you won't have to pay the interest charges that come with an overdraft. What's more, this is not a facility the bank can withdraw and that means that the decision as to whether your business survives or fails is far less likely to be made by someone else!

Of course, some might argue that to sit on cash earning only a small amount of interest is a waste and could be earning you more by investing in more a lucrative project. I'd suggest that this is a very strong reason for holding buffer-funds: so when such an opportunity arises you have the funds ready and available.

But what if you're constantly overdrawn?

Let's say you have an overdraft facility with your bank for £50,000. Only very occasionally do you need the full amount but you never seem to go below £10,000 overdrawn.

What you have here is a long-term borrowing requirement of £10,000, but you're financing it with a bank overdraft facility, which is really designed for short-term needs – and you're paying a premium for the privilege!

The smart move would be to gradually start to build up a buffer-fund to remove the need to borrow that sum at all. Of course, as mentioned above, this might be more of a medium- to long-term solution.

A more immediate step in the right direction might be to seek a term loan; where you borrow a fixed sum now and repay the sum borrowed along with interest over a fixed-term period of (say) two, three or five years.

There are two key provisos here. First, it's only worth doing this if you're planning, at the same time, to arrange to reduce your over-draft facility by the same sum as you've borrowed on your term loan. Thus you're migrating from one loan to another: in effect weaning your businesses off the overdraft to a loan that will eventually be paid off – thus permanently removing your reliance on that portion of your borrowings. Second, this only works if you can a get a loan deal that's not too expensive. Many loan offerings are simply too costly and you'll need to be careful to avoid getting caught with onerous charges and penalties.

The real cost

Watch out, for instance, for how interest rates are quoted. Some lenders will quote a particular rate of interest, which will be applied to the total capital amount initially borrowed each year throughout the period of the loan, irrespective of the fact that each month, due to the payments you make, the amount owed diminishes.

So, on the face of it, the loan on offer may seem to be charging a competitive interest rate when in fact the Annual Percentage Rate (you must have heard the term *APR*) is much higher. I particularly like APR as a measure because it includes *all* costs relating to a loan: not just interest. So whenever you're comparing loans always make sure you determine the APR – other loan cost indicators can be misleading.

Finding an inexpensive term loan which allows you to borrow and then to repay funds over an extended period will lower your costs in the short to medium-term and reduce your level of risk. Although banks have been known to withdraw overdraft facilities at short notice, you're less at risk that this will happen with a term loan – which is more reassuring for you.

Borrowing – the golden rules

1. *Plan ahead and save up to avoid borrowing where possible.*
2. *Only borrow with good reason – just routinely borrowing money is a fool's game – it's expensive and it increases your risk.*
3. *Only borrow to survive a situation you've failed to foresee or to take advantage of an opportunity that won't wait for you to build funds. Remember: that opportunity must be worth it!*
4. *If you are going to borrow then do your research – you may be stuck with this loan for years so it's worth putting in that extra time and effort, on the front end, to make sure you're getting the right deal for your business.*

> *Borrowing money is the smart thing to do...*
> *...ask any commercial lender*

Interest is not the only cost

If a prospective lender tells you their interest rates are highly competitive take a look at the small print of the deal you're being offered and check out all the other ancillary charges that go with it.

These can include setting-up fees, a deposit (which sometimes is not a deposit at all but rather a charge, as the amount you pay isn't repaid!), penalties for late payments, penalties for early repayment of the capital you've borrowed and charges for simply transferring funds from your bank account to repay the loan each month. Be very careful to add these up – the total of such "ancillary costs" can be substantial!

Providers of term loans will (and should) provide you with details of the number of monthly payments and the sum payable for each of them. These are easily checked to determine how competitive this loan is. Here are the steps you can take:

1. *Add up the value of all the payments you make over the whole period of the loan, including any initial charges.*

2. *Subtract from this total the amount you are borrowing – this tells you the total cost of the loan including interest and other charges.*

3. *Divide this figure by the number of years it will take you to pay off the loan – this will give you your cost per year.*

4. *Now divide that cost by half the amount you borrowed and then multiply the result you get by 100 – this gives you a rough average rate of interest (plus related costs).*

*Note: In step 4 we only apply **half** the amount borrowed because over the full-term of the loan only half the initial sum borrowed is owed. After just one month the sum due is reduced and at mid-term only half the capital is still due. Lenders may well present it differently, but the arithmetic is what it is.*

Here's a real life example of a quote provided to one of my clients. His company was suffering cash-flow difficulties and needed to borrow £30,000.

The finance company he applied to (who shall remain nameless) provided him, in essence, with the following quote:

Capital Advance	£30,000
Initial payment	£1,800
Followed by 23 monthly payments of	£1,800

Here's the 4 step calculation:

1. *Total paid over the life of the loan: £1,800 x 24 = £43,200*

2. *Total cost of the loan: £43,200 minus £30,000 = £13,200*

3. *Cost per year: £13,200 / 2(yrs) = £6,600*

4. *Rough average rate of interest and charges:*
   (£6,600 / 15,000) x 100 = 44%

The first thing that struck me about this offer was that although our client was apparently being offered a £30,000 loan, the loan company was taking £1,800 from him before he got it! So the loan was actually only for £28,200. My question to my client was: what part of the statement "I need to borrow £30,000" did they not grasp?

By any reasonable standards, at a rough APR of 44%, this is an outrageously expensive loan. As I recall, when I advised my client not to go for this loan, I may have made reference to *a disinfected bargepole*!

Of course not all lenders are out to rip you off and there are some very good and fair deals to be found. However it's important to realise that there are raw deals out there too and that some well-known High Street brands are not averse to peddling them – take control of your destiny and carefully study the *Ts & Cs...* boring but smart!

Other sources of finance

So far, this chapter has focused entirely on loan finance from banks or other lending institutions, but there are sources of finance which, depending upon your circumstances and the nature of the business you're in, you might feel more appropriate to your needs.

A little help from your friends

One obvious alternative form of short-term funding (to the banks) is, of course, a family member or a friend. If you do go down this route it's particularly important that you view this loan in exactly the same way as you would any bank loan: agree a target date for repayment and plan your cash-flow accordingly.

Don't ever let your lender down; you never know when you might need their help again! Perhaps more significantly, I've seen long-term friendships irrevocably damaged through a failure to repay loans – be careful not to let this happen to any of your cherished friendships.

Sharing the load

In some circumstances it may be a good idea to consider seeking out a partner who will invest in your business. Someone who *invests* is taking a stake or share in the ownership of your business: clearly this is a very different arrangement to that which you'd have with a lender. An investor will not normally be expecting interest payments or repayment of funds injected – though it is possible to have an arrangement where an investment can be *redeemed* at some point in the future.

An ambitious business owner, for example, might seek *capital:* where funds are invested by a specialist venture capital company in return for a financial stake in the business and a say in how it's run – typically there will be a specified target date by which the investment is repaid.

Some business owners are not just looking for a partner who can provide funds: they're looking for someone who can bring much needed expertise to the party too. You may have heard of *Business Angels* who are willing to get involved if they're convinced the proposed business model will work and that they have something different to offer which will significantly help the business.

While bringing in a new investor may appear attractive you must remember you'll now be sharing ownership, which may well mean you will no longer enjoy quite so much freedom in making key decisions and you'll be sharing the financial rewards too. Taking on a business partner is something you should do with the greatest of care; I've seen many such relationships fail with disastrous consequences. The key problem is often more about a clash of personalities than problems with the business itself.

You might consider starting with a trial period to give both parties an opportunity to check how the relationship will work before any permanent commitment is made. It may also be worth, with the help of a commercial lawyer, framing a contract with exit clauses that facilitate less painful separation should problems arise. Such arrangements are easier to agree when the relationship is young and there's plenty of *bonhomie.*

This type of financing can work for you with a careful and sensible approach but you'll need to do your homework on this before you make any legal or financial commitment.

Key points from this chapter

1. Only borrow when you absolutely need to. Lazy thinking causes us to take out loans habitually when in fact we could have avoided the substantial interest and other charges that accumulate over the years, as well as the risk that goes with any borrowing.

2. Think it through carefully before you take out any loan. Are you borrowing for the right reasons? Is it the right type of loan for your needs? Are you confident you'll be able to pay it back?

4. Try weaning yourself off that loans treadmill. Gradually start to build up funds so you can become increasingly less reliant on loans for day-to-day needs.

5. Never rush into any loan – do your research and always read the small print. Simply trusting others not to rip you off is a really bad idea! Where you're absolutely not sure, you must seek independent professional advice.

6. Borrowing from a friend or family member might in some circumstances be a better source of loan funds for you.

7. Bringing in an investor or business partner who can bring something different to the mix can make a huge difference to your business – just make sure the combination of skills, personalities and added funding give you the right blend and that you and your partner agree an exit arrangement that's fair and easy to apply.

CHAPTER NINE

Getting better
all the time

MY ELDEST daughter, an IT Consultant, having spent much time working in and around London, once commented that there were a number of interesting sandwich and deli-style shops near to where she worked but if there was a Subway in the area she'd prefer to go there because you always knew what standard of product and service to expect.

This consistency is powerful stuff, and a principle on which *all* the well-known brands are built. Some brands don't just maintain consistent standards across a whole country; they're able to apply it right around the world in spite of the significant language and cultural differences of the people they employ and serve. So, how on earth do they do it?

You gotta have a system!

There really is only one way to get this level of consistency and that's by employing great systems. By *systems*, we are referring here to a comprehensive set of instructions (or procedures) for doing what you do, to the same, highest possible standards every time, no matter who's doing it or when or where it's being done.

Most small business owners don't truly appreciate the importance and significance of systems in supporting business growth and that's a real shame because, as you will now see, the arguments for using them are really quite compelling...

Your customers will love it

No question, people are far more likely to deal with you if they believe they can trust you. If you prove to them, time after time, that they can rely on you to provide the same high standard of products and services, they are exponentially more likely to keep coming back to you time and time again – and as you should know by now, loyal customers are what great businesses are built on.

> **TIME OUT!**
>
> Many professional practices (eg lawyers, accountants, etc) are prime examples of businesses that *do not* have this consistency. The quality and style of service that a client of one of these practices gets will depend largely upon which partner or employee they happen to get allocated to. The real problem here is that there's no embedded way of doing things throughout an organisation like this – which is a fundamental weakness and undermines the very identity of the business as a whole.

Trust me, customers really, really crave consistency – they want to know that every time they do business with you they're going to receive at least the same high standards of service they received last time, and the time before. If they don't get it, they won't forgive you and they won't stay loyal.

Everyone knows where they are

The very same consistency that your customers crave is also yearned for by your employees. They seek the certainty that they're getting the right result for you and going about it in the right way. In my experience most employees truly want to perform well but very often don't really know or understand what's expected of them.

With effective written systems in place it's so much easier to be clear on what you require of both your new recruits and those more experienced employees who are taking on a new task for the very first time.

This also makes life much easier for you, the owner, needing to delegate a task to someone who has never done it before. Just as important, it introduces a consistency of *"how we do things around here"*. On the one hand you have a happier more confident team working to clear methods and standards and on the other you're enjoying the benefits of knowing that everyone is working to your standards whether you're there or not!

Giving you more time

No doubt about it, systems are a great tool for delegating your workloads to others. Once your system is in place you can delegate more quickly and with greater confidence that everyone around you is working to your standards. What's more if you want to pass some of your workloads to someone who's already overloaded with work, you can use your systems for that person to delegate work too.

It just gets better

When we first started up our accountancy practice, my business partner and I were working hard to set up shop: bringing in new business, coping with the workloads that went with it and sorting out the admin. We were working long hours just to keep our heads above water.

It wasn't until things started to settle down and we recruited our first members of staff that we realised we both had very different ways of working and that it would be highly beneficial for the business as whole if we were to confer and develop an overall scheme of best practice. Without doubt, the resulting systems of working were significantly superior to that which either of us could have achieved on our own. However, it didn't stop there...

As we talked through what would be included in our new improved approach we came up with even more new ideas and some terrific refinements. Looking back we see this now as a major step forward for our business at that time.

What's more it also opened our minds to the potential benefits of constantly moving forward by inviting all our team members to help with the continued development of each and every system we currently follow. We realised that there is no such thing as the perfect approach: there's always scope for making it better.

Our next step was to ask our team to never unquestioningly follow the systems they're given, but to challenge them. Ask why we do it that way and why not try it this way? The benefits of this have been immense as it's not just the intellect of the business owners that have been applied to how we do what we do, but that of all our employees – and over the years they've been coming up with some truly inspirational ideas! And on it goes, *constantly evolving and always getting better.*

I've already referred to the need for ongoing development and growth both on an individual level and for the business as a whole – well thought through systems provide the supporting pillars for consolidating what you already know and continually moving forward from there.

Making your plans a reality

Setting out your plans for the future can be exciting, particularly if they're ambitious and life changing in their nature. However, if you don't convert those plans into specific action steps, you're left with nothing more than a wish list.

If you're a hotelier wanting to set high standards for room cleaning and presentation, a restaurateur wishing to raise table service standards, or an insurance broker seeking to ensure that every time the phone rings, customers get exactly the same high quality experience of dealing with your business – you'll need to specify, in detail, exactly how you wish your people to act... and for that you'll need great systems.

So, systems are not just for carrying out the day-to-day routines; they're an indispensable tool for implementing change effectively, right across the business, and making sure that those changes stick.

Building real value in your business

Many small business owners will, at some point, have in mind a time when they'll wish to sell their business. Perhaps they want to retire or they just feel the need to move on to do something different. Whatever the reason, they'll naturally wish to get the best price they can when they sell and to do this they'll need to offer something that's of real value to the buyer.

Put yourself in the shoes of someone who is looking to buy a business – what would you be looking for? The answer has to be: future earnings – right? You're looking to invest in a business that will give you a level of income that will support the lifestyle you seek. I'm not saying that the assets that come with the business do not hold any value but, mostly, these will only have any significance in that they support the process of generating income.

So if your business has a proven track record of strong profits, that's got to be a big plus, right? It stands to reason that a business with £100K plus profits for the last five years, increasing steadily in that time, will pull a significantly better price than one with declining profits with the latest two years having incurred a thumping trading loss. Even so, on paper your business might be highly successful but if the buyer is being offered no clear systematic approach then the value on offer is much diminished.

Once again look at it from the viewpoint of the prospective buyer: they will be impressed with high profit levels but if they're going to have to work out for themselves how to run the business, they won't feel very confident that they can replicate that performance.

Many small businesses have no written systems in place, with all activities revolving almost entirely around the owner. You could argue, where such is the case, *the owner is the business* for without them it couldn't function in the same way. To be blunt, where this happens there is little intrinsic value to sell beyond the perceived value of its loyal customers. It is therefore crucially important to realise that the real value of your business, should you wish to sell it, is in how well it can function when you're not there!

Great systems form the basis of a "how to" manual for a prospective buyer and the very existence of systems that are being applied on a day-to-day basis by employees, demonstrates your business can and probably does operate, at least to some extent, without you.

If your business can always operate like a well-oiled machine when you're not there, this offers a much more attractive proposition to the prospective buyer – no question!

Common needs

If you are truly serious about growing your business, you cannot ignore the need for written systems for developing an embedded approach that allows you to do everything you do to the very highest standard and to constantly improve and develop.

Can you see the significant differences here between what *you* want from your business and the requirements of a prospective buyer? You shouldn't, there aren't any!

Bottom line: by growing your business for yourself, you're automatically building in additional value for the time when you sell it.

The big names get it

Well-known brand names like McDonald's, Subway and Costa Coffee have all harnessed the power of great systems. The particularly interesting point about these three companies is that they distribute their products through a franchise network.

A franchise exists where a company has a proven, successful business model which it replicates by selling the rights to other businesses, to the same business model commonly in a specific geographic area or "territory". The businesses that buy in to the business model (referred to as franchisees) are tapping in to tried, tested and proven techniques for achieving business success.

In order to achieve that success, the franchisee will need to work to those specific systems that brought success to the franchisor. Without those written systems in place, the franchise would have virtually no value and, more significantly, you may never have heard of some of these world famous brand names.

Writing systems - it's really not that difficult

When you first start to look at developing systems for your business, it may seem like a daunting task but actually it doesn't have to create much more work for you at all – surprised? Read on…

Imagine it's day one for a new recruit to your office and you need to show them an admin task. How do you normally approach it? If you're like most people you'll probably take the new person through a couple of examples and then just let them get on with it: "any problems, come and see me".

Some time later this bright young person has moved on and when another new employee takes their place you go through the same routine again with this and all the other tasks they're going to have to learn, just like their predecessor...

But what if...

OK, here's an alternative approach. Let's say, instead, you provide the first new hire with a writing pad and pen and ask them to take careful notes of the approach you're about to demonstrate and then, when the teaching session is finished, ask *them* to write a system for this task.

Get the idea? *They* are going to write your system – not you! No extra work here for you at all – you were going to show them how to carry out the task anyway – but at the end of this process you'll have a system – which means you'll never have to spend as much time training new employees in the future.

You'll need to review each new system presented to you to make sure it works OK and then once you've done this it just gets added to your ever-growing bank of written systems.

Another advantage here is that the new employee is going to have a much more thorough understanding of the process – they'll have to – as, in effect, they have to explain it in writing and in detail to someone else!

Yet another advantage is that, from this point, in their heart *it's not your system, it's theirs* and if you need to delegate that task elsewhere, who better to teach and train it? Get the idea? Delegating is an extremely important part of the business growth process and here you have a really slick approach to achieving exactly that!

Winning your team over

Some people may hold the view that systems limit an individual's creative abilities; making everyone work in exactly the same way can restrict development.

This argument has some validity where all systems that people work to are hand-me-downs from the boss and where there's no scope for change. This approach does have a somewhat autocratic feel to it and, as a result, can provide an environment that restricts innovation and causes resentment.

If you're going to convince people that this is *not* how it's going to be with systems in your business, you must make it clear on the front end that *they* will be directly involved in developing and maintaining the systems they use.

This means, as it implies, that existing systems are not set in stone; they can and should change when someone comes along with an idea that in some way makes things better. In other words your team members should be encouraged to generate new ideas so that everyone within (and without) the business can benefit! Once people get involved directly in building and improving the systems they work with, they more fully take them on board and truly accept them as the best way to work.

Getting your team even more involved

I rather favour the approach of asking two team members to work together to develop a new system related to what they do.

For instance, someone dealing with customers' requests for information, needs a standard approach in order to guard against the dangers of being too slow in providing a response or failing to get anyone to take responsibility to follow up. In the absence of clear systems this kind of horrendous error can and frequently does occur!

Two people working together can provide a broader perspective and get you a more workable solution at first bite. Handing over responsibility to your team in this way is motivating, not to mention empowering for those involved. Many of the key systems in my firm have been developed in exactly this way.

A system for everything?

Should you have a system for everything you do? No, absolutely not but you do need to cover all the tasks and functions that are critical to the smooth running of the business and in particular, those crucial to how you deal with your customers and prospective customers.

Customers first

When you begin to build your systems I'd start with all customer-facing activities: that way you're creating an underlying consistency to the experience your customers get from dealing with your business.

Tasks as simple as answering the phone are crucially important for the image of your business: how quickly the phone is answered; who answers; how to respond if the caller asks for someone who is not available right now – these all need to be dealt with well and in a consistent way.

Why on earth do we need a system for answering the phone?

This is the incredulous response I've sometimes received from having made this recommendation. However, if you really think about it, an awful lot can go wrong with an incoming telephone call, particularly if your young, inexperienced receptionist had been given no guidance whatsoever.

I've heard of instances where prospective new customers have been greeted with "Hello" instead of an announcement of the name of the business they've called and, when asking to speak with a particular member of staff, being told "he's not in, can you call back sometime?"... ouch!

Of course these are extreme examples but if you're not taking control of this crucially important customer-facing activity you never quite know what any particular individual is going to say – on the other hand I guarantee you'll never have any consistency and occasionally the response the caller gets will be cringe-worthy!

The gradual development of best practice in all those critical areas of the business will make everyone increasingly clearer on how to react, respond and deal with problems and find solutions.

Tasks most likely to go wrong

Some tasks that you could and should delegate may well have wrinkles that make it easy to get it wrong. These are among the tasks that will need your most immediate attention for writing systems.

Of course we humans will always make errors, but we're far less likely to go off track if we have clear written procedures for the best way of doing things. When we do err, building on what we learn from this experience will help guard against repeating the mistakes of the past. The really great thing about systems is that they facilitate this collective, ever-growing knowledge... or should I call it wisdom?

Don't be too ambitious

Certain functions can be so complex that it becomes impossible to write comprehensive systems that cover all eventualities – so don't allow yourself to get too bogged down in that level of detail.

However, you can provide general guidelines regarding the overall approach to be taken, covering the key critical issues that might arise. If you persevere with developing those around you, gradually, they'll better understand what's required and then, in time, you'll be able to trust them to make the right judgments. Until then you may need to maintain close supervision.

Making the right moves

As a schoolboy I was a really keen chess player; a regular member of the school chess club and captain of my school team. At the time I considered myself to be a decent player and decided to join the company chess club when I started my first job.

In my very first game, I played against a reserve player for the third team and I confidently resolved to show just how good I was. You can therefore imagine my utter despair when I found myself totally outclassed! After the game my opponent suggested a couple of books I needed to study if I was really determined to improve my game.

In chess there are so many combinations of moves your opponent can make it's impossible for any expert to give you an effective response to cover every eventuality; a bit like being in business really. However, what an effective book on chess can do is introduce some general principles and techniques – just like systems – which will make you a consistently stronger player.

Even the most highly complex processes will have elements that can be systematised thus making it possible to delegate while consistently maintaining the highest standards of performance.

Look for rules of thumb, or things you've tried and appear to work. Then use your initial notes as a base for future developing and refining. Even though you can't be as prescriptive as you can when setting out systems for dealing with simpler tasks, you can provide yourself and your team with a framework for making consistently smarter moves.

Take care to nurture this most undervalued of assets…

Have you ever heard the term "intellectual property" or "IP"? I'd like you to think of it as a bank of knowledge, unique to your business, which helps it operate more effectively and in some way sets it apart from other businesses. Developing systems in the manner described in this chapter will help you build this very singular asset within your business and may well become its most prized.

Key points from this chapter

1. Do not ignore or underestimate the importance of established, written systems of working for your business – properly written and applied, they can make a massive, positive difference.

2. Writing systems should not be a major task for you. The next time you need to train someone in a particular task, ask that person to make notes and then set up the system for you. There's no additional work for you here: you'd have to explain it all anyway!

3. Most things can be systematised, but not all and not everything needs it anyway. Recognise that certain functions require advanced skills and judgment calls: these can only be effectively applied with the benefit of deep knowledge and experience. Nonetheless, there'll be chunks of even this work that is less skilled and therefore can be systematised and delegated.

CHAPTER TEN

It's a people business

SHORTLY AFTER joining an international shipping group in a senior accounting role, I was taken out for lunch by one the directors. "The shipping business..." he sagely informed me "... is a people business." The strong implication of his remark was that this was something unique to the industry to which he had devoted most of his working life.

Everything I've experienced since that time has convinced me that there's nothing unique about it: all businesses, without any exceptions, are people businesses. No matter how smart you are or hard you work, without people you don't have a business at all. Even if you don't have any employees, you do have customers and suppliers – whatever it is you do, you need to interact with people.

The first really key point to take on board here is that as a business owner you will always need the help and cooperation of others – which means that *you have to deal with and do business with other people.*

The second key point is that if you want get the best out of people then you need to treat them fairly and build their trust. What's more, you need to understand their needs and seek ways to help them fulfil those needs – in a way that fulfils your needs too.

This is not about tricking people or taking advantage of them in order to get what you want but rather (and this is really important) accepting the principle that others have their needs too and that you can get them to serve your needs if you can somehow serve theirs.

This mutuality of benefit is really powerful because when you demonstrate that you care about the needs of other people, they're going to be far more inclined to care about yours – such relationships breed loyalty, trust and a greater willingness to go that extra mile for each other.

Within your growing business your people are your single most important asset – by a long way. Work with them, help them to work well, be on their side and seek to help them to achieve their goals and they will be your most powerful ally.

This chapter looks at the specifics of building those relationships, external to and within your business, which will provide a key foundation for growth. Let's start by looking at some rules for how you treat all those with whom you interact...

Building strong relationships

Trust....worthy

I'm sure you'll agree that for any human relationship to function there has to be some level of mutual trust: the greater that trust, the stronger the relationship. True, there's more to relationships than just this – nonetheless trust is absolutely indispensable.

You can't request it, borrow it or buy it – trust is something you have to earn. If you want people to *truly* help and support you in your endeavours then their trust is a must – but how do you go about building that trust?

When someone first meets you they don't know yet whether they can put their trust in you. It's not that they doubt you, they just don't yet have enough information to have an opinion – but straight away they're looking for signs and the more they get to know you, the clearer the picture becomes.

Integrity

Without even trying we're all quite adept at spotting inconsistencies. If, for instance, you're constantly telling people how you always like to arrive for meetings five minutes early, but consistently turn up 20 minutes late, you're damaging your credibility. Because people rarely say anything when this happens, the guilty party often naively assumes that they haven't noticed – but of course they have and, as a result, trust is eroded.

Real integrity, I would suggest, is the consistency between what you do and what you say you do. When there's a stark disparity between your actions and your words, most people are inclined to believe what they see, which makes your words appear false – not good!

Of course you should always aim to be consistent – if you know you're failing in this area then clearly it's something you need to try and work on. However, if you do find yourself doing this or you're challenged about it, I strongly advise you immediately admit it and apologise. If you try "blanking" it, you erode your credibility even further – big mistake....huge!

It's a fair cop!

If you get something wrong don't doggedly defend your position when it's clear that everyone around you knows you're in the wrong. You're kidding no one except yourself, and in the end you're just undermining their respect for you.

I'm the first to admit this is really tough to do – particularly when pride kicks in or if the person challenging you adopts a bumptious attitude but, believe me, you can deal with the issue more quickly and build respect more effectively by showing your honesty and strength of character.

Working with your team

Feel-good factor

In recent years we've all become more conscious of the need for protecting the health and safety of our employees. Love them or loathe them these statutory regulations, over the last few years, have made the workplace a safer environment.

However, a safe workplace is not automatically a happy one, nor is it one that encourages employees to work at their best. This is not about having state of the art furniture and equipment or a super-duper coffee machine that comes with all the options; it's about providing an atmosphere that supports each and every individual to grow and develop and to help them perform at their best while enjoying a real sense of achievement in doing so.

This approach has to be a win/win for everyone: your employees will be happier and more fulfilled in their work and will be given the scope to continually grow and develop as individuals. Your business benefits as you find it easier to delegate responsibility and business growth is fuelled by the underlying personal growth of the individuals within it. You, as owner of the business, can develop your skills as you let go of more routine and managerial responsibilities and have extra time to acquire the skills you need to take your business forward.

The earlier in the development of your business that you can introduce techniques that will help you provide this positive environment, the more embedded it will be as the business grows. So what steps can you take to achieve all this?

Show you're ready to listen and learn

Have you ever met someone who's never wrong? Everything you say, they have to correct. They're probably listening to what you're saying but only to the extent that it enables them to inform you where you're going wrong. Just a short meeting with a person like this can be irksome and, much worse, life can be hell if this person is your boss. If you're the boss and you exhibit these qualities, your employees aren't always going to complain – but that doesn't mean there isn't a price to pay.

Apart from the very practical argument that you should be making full use of the thoughts and ideas that your people can bring to the table – I'd suggest if you're not open to their views they'll often just shut you out and let you sort out every problem yourself. What a waste!

Be on their side

Regrettably, many business owners and employed managers really are out of their depth when it comes to managing people. Many employees complain that they never really know where they are with their boss; one minute they're best of friends, the next they're grumpy and off-hand.

Worse still is the boss who never compliments you on a job well done; in fact, they never say anything... that is, until something goes wrong, then you're left in no doubt how they feel.

If you're going to be an effective boss you need to be there for your team when they need help. You also need to be prepared to drop whatever you're doing and give them your undivided attention. Make sure they know you want them to succeed and praise them for it when they do – after all, good performance needs to be encouraged – not just greeted with a grunt.

Walk the talk

To win over your team you need to show you really care about them and their needs – I mean *really* care – you can't fake this; believe me if you try to do that, they'll know!

If you do genuinely care about the needs of those who work for you then great, all you need to do now is demonstrate it through your actions. If you don't then I'd advise that you start to nurture within yourself a more considerate way of managing your working relationships – this is not just about being a nice person – it's smart business!

OK, I accept this might be easier said than done, but I put it to you if you do really have a lack of care here it's probably because you're subconsciously seeing your employees' best interests as unrelated to yours; they aren't! The happier and more fulfilled your employees are, the more loyal and supportive they will be and this is so important to every aspect of your business – not just growth but also the smooth running of day-to-day activities and even survival.

Leave your bad moods at home

Ever had a really bad start to the day? You get out of the wrong side of bed having slept badly; you trip over the cat and bump your head – the day's hardly started and you're already fed up. By the time you get into the shower to find there's no hot water you're positively seething and then, just to make your morning complete, the dog bites your foot and you scrape the car on your gateway as you set off to work.

Such ill fortune on the front end of your day is enough to test anyone's patience and hopefully you don't have too many days like this – but this stuff does happen. For whatever reason, there will be times when, arriving at your place of work, you're really not feeling at your best. You must remember however that those people working around you are completely unaware of your problems or concerns – all they see is your behaviour and if they're on the receiving end of your short temper they have absolutely no idea why you are behaving the way you are.

Of course, you don't always act this way, but if you do sometimes then you come across as inconsistent and moody. I've heard colleagues asking each other "What kind of a mood is he in this morning?" when referring to the boss.

In the same way that your customers have a right to expect consistently high standards of service from your business and your people every time, so too are your employees entitled to expect consistent treatment from you – if you can't leave your fluctuating moods outside the workplace you'll undermine all the other good work you may have done in order to foster a great working environment for your team.

So, the next time you're sitting at your desk gingerly feeling the bump on your head and a member of your team approaches you for help, put on a smile to let them know that it's business as usual.

Praise with good reason

The best time to tell someone they have performed well is as soon as you're aware of it. Don't delay, do it immediately. However, don't overdo it – too much praise can come across as insincere and when that happens the message is devalued. The aim here is to positively encourage good performance and to highlight when they've really got it right.

Don't aim to blame

Anyone who has worked in large organisations will have probably endured an environment where managers will look for scapegoats when something goes wrong. A common response to this is for people to stop trying to use their own initiative – they just play it safe.

When the *blame culture* becomes really bad, employees also refuse to think anything through for themselves and just follow orders to the letter. I've even seen office relations so bad that subordinates will only take on something new if they're given written instructions.

The fact is, ultimately, the buck stops with you as the business owner. You need to accept this in its fullest sense – you really do have responsibility to make it all work in your business. Buck-passing is not going to work – if something goes wrong you should, in the first instance, consider carefully what you could have done better. Yes, that's right *you*, not your employee. Look for ways to improve your support of your team and only, in the last resort, if it's clear someone else is really not trying should you ascribe blame on the individual.

Where someone has genuinely tried and failed they should be encouraged to keep on trying and be supported in determining what went wrong so that next time they can get a better result.

Don't forget that running and growing your business is forever a learning process – you will make mistakes – if you're not making mistakes then you're not moving forward. The same goes for your employees – just like you, they are quite capable of coming up with new ideas – you need to nurture that resource not stifle it by having a *mega-strop* every time someone tries something that doesn't happen to work.

Stop the negative behaviour before it starts

Many working environments seem to breed bickering and point-scoring. To be fair, this tends to be more prevalent in the larger organisations, but it can occur too in smaller businesses.

One way to head this off is to get your team together to agree a set of values and behaviours – a list of rules that they sign up and commit to. We've taken this approach in my firm: our small team was given time out from their normal duties to work together to formulate a set of rules that reflected how each individual would want to be treated by their colleagues. Once completed and agreed, this list of "commitments to each other" was posted on the office notice board as a reminder to one and all of how team members should behave towards each other.

Note that this was *not* a set of rules handed down by the boss but rather a reflection of what everyone genuinely felt was fair and reasonable behaviour in the office environment. This process gets people to really think deeply about what is right and fair behaviour towards others and helps to provide a stronger atmosphere of openness and mutual understanding.

Paying your people

Many businesses owners use bonus schemes in specific areas of the business. Typically this can be related to sales and production targets which are easy to quantify, making it simpler to verify performance levels.

I'd suggest that *all* areas of the business can benefit from each and every employee having an element of pay related to performance. Used intelligently, remuneration of all your employees in this way can help to control both the *quantity* and *quality* of the work your people carry out.

Promoting great performance

Of course, some roles within a business lend themselves more easily than others to determining performance. The sales person, for instance, either reaches their sales quotas or doesn't – but what about the cleaning staff; how do you assess and reward their good work?

Further, it's crucially important to recognise that no roles can be fairly assessed on the basis of quantity alone – quality is just as important. However, if you really think about it, this is even true for the sales person: if they achieve exceptionally high sales this month but sell to customers who have a reputation of never paying up, then they're not really working in the best interests of the business.

It follows therefore that you need to be clear, in your own mind, what good performance looks like and then reward on the basis of actual performance compared to that standard. For instance, you may wish to reward your sales person based on payments your business receives from customers rather than the sales invoices generated – this will motivate them to sell more responsibly. Also if you were to give the sales person the power to offer discounts to customers, you might consider it a good idea to base their commissions on profit margin rather than the full selling price. These carefully constructed refinements of the rewards you offer can help to ensure that when your people achieve their goals and targets, they're achieving yours too!

Assessing the performance of cleaning staff may well also have both quantitative and qualitative elements. Quantitative issues may include setting targets for keeping cleaning materials costs down while qualitative might include following strict standards according to written procedures, accompanied by occasional reviews to assess performance.

I've provided these two examples partly to show that, no matter what the role, linkage between pay and performance can be made to work for your business and also to demonstrate that there really is no good reason to pay *any* employees a flat-rate wage. As we all know from experience, there are some people who don't need any motivation whatsoever – they'll work their socks off for you no matter how much (or little) you pay them. However, even these people aren't always working in your best interests. A carefully constructed bonus system combined with clear goals, standards and systems will help you multiply your own efforts many times over – you've got to admit this is powerful stuff!

I'd suggest that a significant proportion of each of your employees' pay should be performance related. If you're only going to pay them an extra "tuppence" for achieving the very important goals you've set, then you're not being serious about making it work for your business.

How you approach this will depend on the responsibilities ascribed to each employee and the nature of the work they are required to do. Some of our clients, for instance, at the most basic level, employ a fixed salary element broadly equal to the national minimum wage but with a significant extra bonus on offer based on performance.

Here are some important ground rules for your bonus system…

Give them the power

First, you do need to be absolutely sure here that your employee is completely in charge of their own destiny. In other words there's no point in giving someone responsibility for something over which they have no or only limited control. *Responsibility and authority must go together in equal measure.* Your people need to be given complete control over those responsibilities they are required to fulfil in order to achieve their rewards. What's more you will need to be sure they fully accept that this is so – otherwise their motivation will be seriously undermined.

Combine and rule

Also be careful to avoid conflict. For instance, if you were to provide your production team with responsibility for maximising output only and give someone else responsibility for quality, you're asking for fireworks. I'd suggest all roles need some balance between qualitative and quantitative measures at least wherever possible. Best practice is to work with each of your employees to set out performance standards – just imposing your ideas is never going to work so well. Your people really need to believe that the tasks they are being set are worthwhile and achievable – if not then they're not going to be motivated to work to your standards.

Nice and easy does it

This is likely to be something that many employees have never experienced so you'll need to careful here and gently introduce the idea of linking pay to performance. Show the benefits of this approach to them and explain clearly how they can earn more than they would on a fixed wage – if they perform to required standards. I'd also suggest you look to introduce the process slowly and above all incrementally, gradually bringing a larger proportion of total pay linked to performance.

Make time to save time

Does all this seem like a lot of hard work and fuss? No question you will need to put some thought and effort into setting up these systems but once you've done it, it will pay you back many, many times over.

Although it's many years ago now, I can recall my school lessons in science where we were shown how, using levers, you could lift loads that would otherwise be immovable. This "leverage" allows us to multiply what we could otherwise achieve, many times over. If you think about it, putting time in to harnessing the energies of your team is much like employing those levers; you are, in effect, serving to multiply the effect of your efforts. Far from being wasteful, I cannot conceive of a more effective way of investing your time!

Of course, you have to put all the hard work in on the front end and it may well be some time after you've completed the process that you start to see the fruits of your efforts but there can be no doubt that in the long run this has potentially life-changing payback for you as the business owner. The benefits that can accrue from just working, on your own, on the day-to-day routines, pale into insignificance compared to this!

In reality this is pretty much true for all the business development work you do, so if you can take on board this principle and work with it, it will bear fruit for you well beyond anything you can achieve through just plodding along and hoping for the best.

Key points from this chapter

1. People are a fundamental requirement of your business. The better your working relationships the stronger and safer your business will be.

2. To build strong working relationships you must build trust. If people trust you they will happily work with you and more readily support you in what you're trying to achieve.

3. You can build that trust by demonstrating that you do what you say you will do and that you can be relied upon to keep your promises and live up to your commitments. If you don't, people might not say anything... but they'll know and they won't trust you.

4. Show that you're looking for mutual benefit: that you're willing to give as well as take.

5. Move away from paying your employees the same fixed wage irrespective of performance. Reward them for helping you to achieve your goals, which is the true definition of good performance. Make sure they're clear what good performance looks like and then help them to achieve it.

CHAPTER ELEVEN

When the going gets tough

MOST BUSINESS owners will, at some time, face challenges that threaten the very existence of their business. These can be stressful times and sometimes in spite of their best efforts it can all end in disaster.

Much of the material in this book is aimed at strengthening your business, thereby helping you to avoid disasters and put yourself in a better position to deal them with when they do arise. There's a strong underlying message here: *the application of business development techniques are not solely aimed at growing your business, they're also a very crucial aid for business survival!*

None of us is immune to getting caught out by a sudden and unexpected turn of events and, when this happens, things can spin out of your control with alarming speed. In this chapter we're going to take a look at some typical problems that can arise, what defences you can put in place in advance and how you'll need to respond when your business suddenly faces a crisis.

What can possibly go wrong?

The short answer to this question is: just about anything! Business is complicated and very dynamic: things are changing all the time and they're doing it quicker now than they've ever done in the past. That said, it's quite easy to define the scope of what you're dealing with when things start to go badly wrong.

Let's keep it simple…

While no one can accurately foretell what serious challenges your business will face, I can confidently predict that it will affect only two aspects of your business: profitability or cash-flow… or both. You may well meet challenges that don't affect either of these but they're not going to be life-threatening to your business.

From this simplified viewpoint it's possible to layout some general ground rules which will help you survive the initial storm and, by so doing, provide your business with that precious time you'll need to identify and deal with the real underlying issues that brought about your misfortune in the first place. Let's first look at how you can toughen your business up so it's less vulnerable to those unpredictable events…

Having your defences in place

There's nothing you can do to give yourself complete protection against serious business problems. Nonetheless, there are steps you can take to significantly reduce the likelihood that they will occur and, what's more, those same steps will put your business in a much stronger position to survive if they do.

In fact the whole content of this book is geared to providing you with the wherewithal to do just that. *Virtually all the growth techniques covered in these pages apply equally to strengthening your business* so you're better prepared for the tough times.

Here's a summary of specific steps you can take to strengthen the defences of your business against those major threats:

1. **Run your business in growth mode.**

   Even if you're not interested in growing your business, you need to seek some level of constant forward motion. Remember it's very difficult for your business to stand still – it's either going forward or going back. If you're always on the front foot you have to be in a much stronger position to deal with the problems that land on your plate.

2. **Build your own strengths**

   *When your business is up against it, it's down to you to sort it out. The stronger your business knowledge and experience, the better your chances of survival. Taking the view that **I'll cross that bridge when I get to it** is naïve and reckless when you've got a mortgage to pay.*

3. **Build strong relationships with your customers**

   You need their loyalty and by showing them that you can serve them well and that they can trust you, they'll be more forgiving when things go wrong and are far more likely to stay with you when your business is faced with increased competition.

4. **Build strong relationships with your suppliers**

   Show them they can trust you by rewarding their good service, staying loyal and demonstrating that they can rely upon you to keep your promises. Then, when times get rough, they're far more likely to support you and see you through.

5. **Build strong relationships with your employees**

   If they believe in you and what you're doing they're more likely to stay with you and support you when you need them most.

6. **Build a strong and broad repertoire of marketing techniques**

   These will be methods of lead generation and sales conversion that are currently working for you. Having a broad range of these techniques, means that when one of them stops working for you, you'll have many others to support your sales revenues.

7. Maintain an emergency fund

Trust me, there'll be a time in the future when you'll be glad you did this (or dearly wish you had!). This contingency fund could well be the difference between survival and failure.

I've often been asked what level of funds should be held for emergencies. Given that, when facing disaster, you need to buy yourself more time I'd suggest a fund equal to two months' worth of your business outgoings should do it. This may seem like I'm over-egging the pudding here, but it might not feel that way when you're in the eye of the storm!

8. Maintain a *reserve* **bank overdraft facility**

This is a credit facility you're not using but that's there should you need it. If it's already in place when your business hits the buffers, you won't need to go cap in hand to your bank manager. Also, there's no wasted time trying to find that urgently needed extra finance – believe me, you'll have enough on your plate without burning up valuable time chasing loan facilities you should have had in place already!

9. Keep a close eye on profits

You must make a profit on each unit of product or item of service you sell. Equally you need to sell in sufficient volumes, first to cover all your fixed costs and then to make a profit. If you don't know how profitable your business is right now, how can you be sure you're not already sustaining losses?

One of the most common causes of business failure is a significant decline in profits – if you've got your eye on the ball here you should identify the problem at an early stage thus giving yourself more time to act before it all gets too serious.

10.Make provisions for future known expenditure

If you know years, or even months, in advance of major expenditures on the way or taxes due, why would you just wait for it to happen and then try to borrow the necessary funds? Better to build your funds as you go along. This will save you money and help to avoid short-term cash-flow shortages.

11. *Avoid over reliance on borrowing*

A large amount of debt commits you to relatively large interest payments, which can cause cash-flow and profitability problems to be far more acute in the bad times. When times are tough this is one outgoing you can't cut back on!

12. *Never allow too much credit to any one customer*

An obvious rule, but one so often ignored in the chase for maximising sales. A customer who fails to pay £100 can cause you irritation but one who fails to pay you £100,000 may cause your business to fail – you can't predict the outcome but you can limit your exposure.

13. *Keep hold of the reins*

Keep a constant and careful eye on how well your business is performing in terms of your cash reserves and your borrowing – never lose sight of where you are at any point in time. If you do then you're leaving your very livelihood to chance.

14. *Keep your eyes peeled*

Stay sensitive to what's going on within your business and in the environment in which your business has to operate. It stands to reason, if you walk around with your eyes shut, eventually you'll bump into something!

Circling the wagons

In spite of your best efforts, serious problems can sometimes be completely unavoidable. When you are faced with a challenge to the very existence of your business, you have to deal with it effectively and quickly – but where do you start? What follows is a set of guidelines designed to help you get immediate clarity on the nature of the problem, set out the steps you need to take to deal with it and show you how to prioritise your efforts...

Getting a grip

When the guano hits the fan, it's down to you to sort it out. Don't waste time griping about your ill luck or asking yourself *why me?* You need to accept responsibility, not only for your current fix but also for taking an immediate and firm grip on the problem.

One very, very common error is to ignore it and convince yourself the problem will sort itself out in time. Believe me this is a very bad idea. If you leave a problem to fester, guess what happens... yep, that's right, it festers, transforming from a relatively small problem into a potential catastrophe.

Eventually, you're going to have to face the problem, the earlier you do so the less serious it's likely to be and the more time you'll have to put things right. Surely it's far better to deal with any problem *as soon as it arises, on your own terms* rather than ignoring it and then having to face a far more serious and urgent crisis, further down the line.

Once you've realised you have a serious problem you're going to need to devote a reasonable chunk of your time, in the short run, to attending to survival issues – however you still have a business to operate and customers to serve so you need to maintain a healthy balance between the two. Where practicable put all other issues on the back burner.

Be open to possibilities...

Just because you can't immediately think of a solution to a particular problem, it doesn't mean there isn't one – take the positive view that there is a way through this and that it's just a matter of looking at it objectively. Also, getting the comments of others will give you a different perspective that, very often, will not have occurred to you.

Like so many things in life it's about getting a balance – keep an open mind to what others have to say – listen particularly to the views of those whose opinions you trust but don't completely close your mind to any relevant comments that come your way. Ask yourself: how can I use this? Can I apply it to my business? Even if I can't apply it to this specific problem can I develop it in some way or can I apply it in some other way that can be beneficial?

So, what's the problem?

When faced with impending disaster it's easy to become beset by feelings of confusion and despair. If you find yourself in this state of mind, you need to realise, on the front end, that it's your confusion and an initial lack of clarity regarding what the underlying problems are that can bring about that despair.

So, as your first step, you need to define your problems and clarify the order in which you need to deal with them. For instance you may have just realised that profits have declined and because no immediate action was taken you now have a cash-flow problem too. If you don't have sufficient funds to pay suppliers, they won't supply you and, therefore, your business can no longer function.

Obviously you'll need to address that profitability issue fairly quickly but your most pressing challenge is to ensure that your business has funds sufficient to enable it to keep trading for now – this will then give you some breathing space to work out the reasons why you've got a cash-flow problem in the first place.

You need to set out a plan of action, along with further contingency plans, should that plan fail.

Divide and conquer

Sometimes the problems facing you can appear overwhelming. It's at times like these you need to remember that large, complicated problems are best dealt with by breaking them down into more manageable chunks and dealing with each of those chunks, one at a time. The order in which you attack them should depend upon how time critical each of them is to your business survival and which other chunks depend upon them.

Be mindful of the time you've got

The root cause or causes of your problem may be easily identifiable or it may take some work to get to grips with. Once you have determined the underlying causes you'll need to set out action steps to put it right and this all takes time.

How much time you have will depend on your cash reserves. If you have none then you really are under pressure to turn things around quickly. If, for instance, the reason for your business difficulties is that you're not generating sufficient sales, there are action steps you can take to turn things around, but if you've completely run out of cash to pay your suppliers then you no longer have the means to trade. As we've already seen, you can survive in the short-term without making profits but you'll quickly hit a brick wall without cash. For this reason you're going to need to work firstly on maximising your cash reserves and the credit available to your business.

Building trust and obtaining credit

As already discussed, a lack of cash is never the root cause of business failure – it's simply a consequence. Nonetheless, it's very often an insufficiency of funds that brings a failing business to its final breath. More specifically, the business usually seizes up because unpaid creditors at some point say *enough is enough* and refuse to supply until payment is made.

In practice, however, the creditors' real reason for stopping credit commonly has more to do with a loss of trust than the amount of debt outstanding. This is because the owners of cash-strapped businesses often chronically mismanage their relationship with their suppliers – you need to take care not to make the same error.

Some common and seriously unwise responses to communications from concerned suppliers include ignoring supplier statements and demands (some business owners feel so uncomfortable about their situation they don't even open the mail!) and not taking or returning calls from worried creditors.

Charm offensive

Trade credit is an extremely important source of finance, therefore your relationship with your suppliers is, equally, of paramount importance; the last thing you want to do is damage it. So, as soon as you realise you absolutely can't pay your creditors in accordance with previously agreed terms *you need to step up your communication with them, not shut it down.* Yep, that's right; it's time to get on the phone (or better still, go and meet with them) and explain the situation, apologise for the inconvenience and offer to pay *all* the sums outstanding in accordance with a mutually agreed schedule. *Never* leave doing this until you're getting stroppy letters – by that time the damage has been done!

WHY?

This discussion, with your creditors, has three key purposes:

1. *To reassure your suppliers that you have every intention of paying them: this way they're not wasting their time having to chase after you for money. You want them on your side not working against you and, just as importantly, you need your working relationship with your suppliers to remain intact for the long run.*

2. *To give you more time to pay, which, in turn, will allow you more time to deal with the problems you face.*

3. *To save yourself more time by cutting out the hassle you'll get if you haven't got your suppliers' understanding and cooperation.*

What should your approach be?

I'd suggest you plan out your proposed payment schedule very carefully. Give yourself as much time to pay the backlog of debt as possible.

If you want to protect your relationship with your suppliers you need to be absolutely certain that you keep your side of the bargain and make your scheduled payments when you say you will. So when you're setting out your schedule you need to be sure that what you're committing yourself to is well within your financial capabilities.

If you wish to maintain your credibility, the last thing you need is to have to renegotiate in a couple of months' time because you find you can't make the payments you'd agree to. If, further down the line, you're able to pay off the outstanding debt more quickly, then you can unilaterally step your payments up.

From this point your key aim should be, at least, to honour your promises and maintain trust.

Who should you approach in this way?

When you're faced with serious cash and credit problems you're likely to find that much of your time is soaked up in crisis management – so it's important to manage your time well.

I'd suggest you focus your attention primarily on those to whom you owe most and/or are most critical to your trading supplies. Suppliers to whom you owe smaller amounts, if you can, should be just paid off – often there are far more of these but, in total, of less financial significance. The last thing you need is dozens of suppliers breathing down your neck; you may as well narrow it down to just that small number of suppliers to whom the lion's share of debt is owed.

With the right approach, dealing with your suppliers openly and honestly will maintain their trust. This in turn will help rather than hinder you in your quest for business survival and once your crisis is passed, you'll be able to continue trading with key relationships intact.

Does this approach work every time, with all suppliers?

Regrettably you'll always get the difficult individuals who will be inflexible however honest and communicative you are: however, you'll find that overall most people will respond positively when treated openly and honestly in this way.

Dealing with those intransigent individuals who won't negotiate and demand immediate full settlement is more challenging. If you can I'd suggest you try to pay these people off to get rid of the hassle. However, you'd be wise to take note of those you can and cannot rely upon when times are tough. Perhaps you need to ask yourself, when things have settled down once again, whether it's worth continuing to deal with people who will kick you when you're down.

Other cash sources

You can, among other actions, increase your cash by reducing debtors and stock and applying for sources of credit other than trade credit. For help on improving your management of these potential cash sources, refer to Chapters 7 and 8.

A loan to tide you over

You can, of course, give yourself more time by arranging a temporary increase in your bank overdraft facility or by taking out an additional loan. It is, however, one of the ironies of the commercial world that lenders are often least inclined to loan you funds at the very point you need them most. So, in difficult times, you may find additional loan facilities a little thin on the ground. That said, it's certainly wise to seek out additional sources of funds if you don't already have contingent loan facilities in place.

Whatever action you decide to take regarding additional loans, you need to carefully think through your actions. Clearly it's a really bad idea to blindly borrow funds without having a plan for repaying them. It would also be irresponsible to take on new loans if you do not truly believe you can overcome the problems you face.

The root of the problem

Once you've given yourself some breathing space, it's now time to turn your attention to identifying and effectively dealing with the root cause of the challenges you face. If you've simply got cash-flow problems and you don't know why, the chances are there'll be strong clues in your accounts. Whenever a bewildered small business owner tells me they're short of cash but don't know the reason, I normally suggest we look at the most common underlying causes...

Are you making a profit?

This is pretty obvious question to ask. If your business is making a loss then your cash is going down a plughole. I'd suggest this has to be where you begin your investigations. Sadly, for many cash-strapped business owners, this would be the last place they'd look!

If you're unsure whether or not your business is making a profit then you need to find out, without delay! If you don't feel confident you can accurately work this out for yourself, call your accountant, explain the problem and ask them to help you determine your current level of profitability. *Do it now!*

If you do determine that your business is currently incurring losses, you need clarity on why and what has changed. Only then can you start to put in place a plan of action. Whatever other problems your business has, you can't ignore this for very long. Answering the following questions will help you here:

1. *Have your sales volumes gone down?*

2. *Has the profit margin on the sales you make declined?*

3. *If your profit margins have gone down – what's changed? Have you been cutting your prices? Have your direct costs gone up? If so, which ones and why?*

4. *Have your overhead costs increased? Once again, if so, which ones and why?*

Assess the overall effect of your findings to determine if one or a combination of the above issues has contributed to bringing you to where you are.

Even if you determine for sure that profitability is a key cause of your current situation, it may nonetheless be worth reviewing the other areas covered below. If profitability has not changed then you'll need to carry on searching for the answers anyway.

Are you taking too much out of your business?

If your business is making a loss then, if you haven't already done so, you must face the harsh reality that for now you shouldn't be drawing out any cash for yourself at all.

I've often received a very annoyed response from clients when I've pointed this out in the past: "What am I supposed to live on?" Sorry guys, if cash isn't being generated by the business in the first place, drawing it out is madness!

Of course, the same principle applies when your business is making profits but where you're drawing more out than it's generating – doing it occasionally you might get away with, but to do so routinely is simply not sustainable! So carefully compare cash-profits (not forgetting taxes!) generated by your business with what's being drawn out. If you're over-drawing you need to take remedial action and quickly.

How much do your customers owe you?

The total sum owed to you by your customers at any point in time can create a big hole in your finances. Of course the provision of credit to your customers, for many industries, is perfectly normal and, if correctly managed, will not cause serious problems.

However, if the amount of credit allowed is not properly controlled, with customers being allowed extended periods before being pressed for payments or just allowed too much credit at any one time, this can cause a dangerous drain on cash resources.

The good news is, it should be easy to check what your current total trade debtors figure is. If you've been operating a standard accounting software package you can check back over the past few months to determine whether or not there has been an upward trend. If there has and that increase is significant then straight away you've found one (if not the only) reason for your cash-flow difficulties.

Another point of comparison is the trade debtors figure calculated by your accountant when they prepared your most recent set of annual accounts.

If your investigations do show a significant increase in trade debtors, then you need to determine why. Start by looking at who owes you most, try to identify what's changed and then follow it up with remedial action. For detailed help on how to get a grip on your trade debtors see Chapter 7.

Are you still taking credit from your suppliers?

Just like allowing trade credit to your customers, making use of credit offered by your suppliers is a normal part of trading but if you're not seeking credit and simply paying all or most of your expenses immediately they become due, this is going to have a significant, negative effect on the amount of cash you hold at any point in time.

You'll need to check whether the amount of credit you're taking has fallen significantly during the period since your cash-flow started to decline. If it has then this too could be a major contributor to your overall cash-flow problem. For more help with managing trade credit see Chapter 7.

Have you got too much cash tied up in stock?

Some businesses carry huge amounts of stock (inventories) and often quite unnecessarily tie up a large amount of precious cash that could perhaps be used more profitably elsewhere in the business.

This process is about identifying what's changed, what's caused your cash reserves to decline – could it be that you're now carrying more stock than you have in the past? If the answer is yes, you need to determine why and take action. Look out, in particular, for any accumulation of *obsolete* stock lines – these can lead to a massive drain on your cash reserves.

Consider trying to sell off this stock even if it is at a significantly knocked-down price – if it is truly obsolete anyway you may as well accept the loss and convert it into as much cash as possible in order to ease your current cash shortage. For guidance on steps you can take to better manage your stocks see Chapter 7.

Is your business expanding?

If your sales are increasing and you're having to pay out extra cash to fuel your growing business this can be a huge drain on your finances.

Business journalists have often commented upon the irony that one of the most common times for business failure is when an economy is just coming out of recession. It works this way because during an economic downturn, when there's a lot of uncertainty, people stop spending. When things start to improve, though, people start making the purchases they've been holding back on for so long it's like opening up the floodgates! So, all of a sudden the order books start to fill and businesses are working flat-out to cope with the sudden surge in demand. At this time profits are looking good but because so much is ploughed into servicing customer needs, businesses start running low on cash – and when that happens they become extremely vulnerable.

If you've been expanding your business and you've got chronic cash-flow problems, the two could well be related. When this happens, what do you do? As referred to above, you need to fill that cash gap. Business expansion needs to be properly financed and that means planning for it before it gets to a point when it's a problem.

If you can't get the loan you need quickly enough then you may need to consider slowing down on your expansion to give your cash some time to catch up. It's never easy to turn business away, I know, but if it's the only way to avoid disaster then this may be your best way forward.

What about major purchases?

At times when you have some spare cash you're more likely to get tempted into buying that large item of equipment you've been promising yourself for some time. If you succumb to this there's always the danger you'll be using up cash you'll need for other purposes at some point in the near future.

Have you made any major purchases in recent months and paid out a large lump sum? If you have, this could well be one reason for your current cash-flow dilemma.

While you can't undo this error you might consider seeking "asset finance". This is a kind of loan facility that links security, for the lender, to the asset you bought. With some assets you can sell them to specialist finance companies who will lease them back to you. This is not always the cheapest form of finance, but it may be a way out of your immediate predicament.

Getting expert help

If you're not able to answer any the above questions for yourself or the answers you've come up with thus far have failed to unearth the real source of the problem, I'd suggest you seek some expert advice from your accountant. They'll be able to read your financial numbers with greater ease and speed than you and will be in a much stronger position to identify underlying problems. If your accountant tells you they can't help, find a new one and quickly!

From defence to attack

You've identified the problem – now what?

Once identified, you'll need to set out a plan of action for remedying the underlying problems you face. Most likely, your findings will identify something you've missed in the management of your business or something you've not done. The preceding chapters of this book provide much of the key material you'll need to remove those critical weaknesses and get you back on track.

Plan B mentality

Dropping a paperclip on the floor is no big deal; you just pick it up – no need for any contingency plans here. On the other hand a major meltdown of the reactor at a nuclear power plant could cause a disaster of cataclysmic proportions – so built-in safety devices are of vital importance.

That's why, where nuclear power plants are concerned, having a warning device in place to ensure that operatives are aware if a meltdown kicks off would seem a sensible precaution... but what if that device malfunctions? The smart move would be to set up a second device, operating completely independently from the first, so even if the first fails the second will give a warning anyway.

The chance of both devices failing is very small but not impossible so a third device is put in place to raise the alarm in times of impending disaster. Get the idea? If it's critically important that your endeavours succeed it's worth putting in place as many contingency plans as possible – so, whatever your escape plans are, you're keeping your chances of failure to an absolute minimum.

So, you need to carefully seek out your best plan of action and once you've set it in motion, immediately seek out a Plan B because, who knows, your initial approach might not work. If your business depends on sorting a particular problem out then a Plan C is also advisable.

Facing the harsh reality

I've encountered businesses where the owners just can't find a way forward but with some expert help and guidance have been able to change their fortunes. I've also seen hard-working, diligent business owners fail to turn their business around no matter what they tried. They're not to blame; the fact is some business models, particularly where something fundamental has changed, simply can't be made to work anymore.

An obvious example of this has been demonstrated on British high streets. Gradually, in recent years, many small retail businesses have been squeezed out by increased competition from large retail chains, out-of-town shopping malls and from rising rental charges and business rates. Once highly profitable businesses fail because a business model that once worked, sadly, no longer does.

Adapt or bust

It's vital that you recognise when this kind of commercial *tsunami* is heading your way. Carrying on doing what you've always done in the past and hoping for the best is not a great option. Business survival depends on you becoming proactive and *changing your game.* This is not admitting failure, it's part of the natural process of adapting to the world around you – we all have to do it on some level.

If you realise, at a late stage, that the fundamentals of your business aren't working anymore and perhaps haven't been working for some time, then you need to be very clear on how you're going to turn things around. No doubt about it, you're going to have to make some major changes to the way your business operates and you'll need to do it in short order.

Taking the actions outlined above to improve your cash-flow in the short-term will certainly help provide you with more time to turn things around. However, if the way your business operates is fundamentally flawed, these palliative techniques will do no more than delay the inevitable. You *must* therefore identify a way forward that will remove those key flaws.

The harsh reality is that if you can't find a way forward then there's really no point in blithely carrying on and delaying the inevitable. When you realise that the business has no viable future you may as well call it a day now rather than waste more of your time and money. This doesn't mean you need to quit running your own business... just this business.

The savvy business owner isn't immune to problems of this nature, but they won't wait for events to overtake them, they'll act quickly, decisively and move on. When you find yourself in this situation you should do the same.

Key points from this chapter

1. If you've got a serious problem in your business, it's either directly affecting profit or cash... or both!!

2. To improve chances of survival get your defences in place – most of the techniques in this book will help you to do exactly that!

3. Act quickly, as soon as you're aware there's a problem – don't let it fester. That way you'll be more in control and able to deal with the problem on your own terms.

4. If you have a cash-flow problem right now, you need to deal with that first. Once you've obtained additional cash funds to keep you going for now you can then concentrate your efforts on identifying the source (or sources) of the problem.

5. Your financial records will be a key source of information when seeking answers to your current dilemma. If you're not confident you can do this yourself, get help. Your accountant has the skills to help you identify where things are going wrong.

6. Once you've identified the problem set out your plan of action. When your business is struggling to survive it's critically important that your plan works – but what if it doesn't? Answer: always have a Plan B and even a Plan C.

7. If your investigations identify fundamental weaknesses in your business model then you must open your mind to sweeping changes in the way you operate and even to the possibility that you're no longer in the right business!

CHAPTER TWELVE

Pulling it all together

IN THE first chapter, you will recall, I posed the question "What are the key ingredients of business success?" Everything that followed has been aimed at answering this crucially important question. For many of us *success* is something that stands off somewhere in the distant future: it's a major event or milestone that will take a long time to reach, perhaps months or even years from now.

The downside of this view is that it often leaves us with a feeling of discontent – a sense that we won't really be happy or fulfilled until we achieve our ultimate goals. In a way this is a bit like we're living our lives in an airport lounge – constantly on our way to somewhere else, without ever truly feeling we've *arrived* or any real contentment with where we are right now, in this moment.

I'd like to challenge that view. In fact I would strongly suggest that with any major success you have in business or in life, it is never one single event that brings it about but rather it's an accumulation of lots of smaller successes you've achieved over a far longer period of time.

Sadly, at the time they occur, these many successes seem so minor and insignificant, we fail to celebrate or even acknowledge them: nonetheless without them the big wins cannot happen! Every single one of those small wins takes you one step closer to your ultimate goals. Have you achieved one of these today? If so, your success is right here and now, not some time in the future. In essence, if your business is constantly moving forward, with one small success after another, then *you're succeeding right now*!

I'm not suggesting you should be content with where your business is at this point in time but you have every right to feel satisfied and comfortable with your current forward motion if it's taking you on your chosen path. *You're in success mode – it's a good place to be.*

> *Success is not something that only occurs when you reach your destination...*
>
> *... it's happening with every single step along the road.*

The smallest unit of success is that easy to take bite-sized step. It's something you can do today, right now, and it's your first of many.

The savvy way

You'll need to patiently apply each of your small steps to a combination of activities within your business and if you really are going to make things better you'll need to recognise and apply those "golden threads" that characterise the *savvy small business.*

Let's now pull together those key *threads*:

It really is all about you

Your business is a reflection of you. If you're not developing and growing then neither is your business. Not every small business owner ambitiously seeks stellar business growth, but in my experience, most are looking for a better deal than they're currently getting. Low income, no spare time, lack of holidays, too much daily hassle and a general feeling of financial insecurity are common complaints of many people I speak to.

If you're seeking a better deal then you have to be prepared to learn and develop ways of working that best serve your needs. This requires your complete acceptance that from now on your business is a learning process. In all your endeavours you should be constantly asking yourself: *Is there a better way?*

Development techniques are relevant to you

It doesn't matter whether you're seeking to build your business into a multimillion pound enterprise or just feel the need to give yourself a little more financial security, the tools and techniques you'll need to employ are largely the same. The difference in outcome for you will depend more upon how much time and effort you're prepared to put in.

The John Lewis Partnership and Marks and Spencer have to face exactly the same commercial realities as your corner shop: they must provide products or services that appeal to the customer and they must constantly adapt and grow. True, they are large organisations now but, like your business, they started small and they didn't get to where they are now by ignoring the need to develop. Along the way both of these companies have had to face major challenges: if they'd been completely unprepared or unable to deal with those challenges they probably wouldn't be around now.

Set your course and stick to it

The savvy business owner knows where they want to be, sets their course and lays out their specific action steps. As they proceed along their path, they will encounter many distractions but will not allow these to push them off course.

You have to be single-minded in this way. Constantly refer to your written plans and values and make sure that each and every thing you do is taking you where you wish to go. This is what true leadership is.

Apply the massive power of combination

Each of the techniques and tools in this book and those you will develop yourself can, individually, have a powerful, positive effect on your business – but applied in combination the effect can be truly enormous!

Consider for one moment… The introduction of systems for properly managing your pricing means you get the best return on the products and services you produce, improve profitability and cash-flow… Setting up systems for proactively managing debtors will save you a huge amount of hassle and time and this will also help cash-flow too… Employing someone who is efficiently trained using your systems which will then free up your time so you can generate more income than that employee is costing you and will also increase profitability and, once again, improve cash-flow…

See how these very different techniques overlap and reinforce each other? The combined power of these techniques can be huge – what difference would it make to your business if you were to tap into the many techniques now available to you?

Marketing – make it part of everything you do

For your business to function effectively you must connect with your customers. To simply hope that your products and services are what your customers need, without proactively consulting with them, will cause you to waste much time, effort and money.

If you're seeking to improve business performance then you have to accept that a good deal of your time and energies will need to be dedicated to effective two-way communication with your target customers. You have to learn from them what their needs and concerns are and show them how your products or services can meet those needs.

Accept that a good deal of your own learning process will relate specifically to this area; dedicate time to it and gear all your business activities to serving your customers.

Everything you sell has to be worth it

You must never forget that the fundamental purpose of your business is to serve your customers. Get this wrong and you'll fail but getting it right is no guarantee of success.

Once you've found a product or service that ideally meets your customers' needs, it is only worth marketing, producing and delivering if your customer will pay you a price that will give you the profit you need. If you can't strike a price that is attractive to both you and your customers then you must either find a way to improve the deal or walk away!

Always keep track of profits

Too many businesses don't know how much profit they've made until some time after the end the year when their accountant tells them. This is no way to run a business! Not only do you need to know, broadly, how much profit you're making each week or month – you must be clear on how much you're making on each sale. If you don't know this, how can you be sure you're not making a loss? If you're going to take control of your business you absolutely cannot afford to leave your profits to chance.

Cash-profit is King!

I'd suggest that you haven't really made a profit on any sale until you've got paid for it. The tax inspector and even your accountant may disagree with this point of view, but the fact is you can't spend profit... only cash.

If you need to pay the bills, buy that new piece of equipment or draw money out of the business for yourself, you'll need to constantly generate a cash surplus. The main source of your cash surplus can only be profits, but profit in itself is no good to you unless you convert your profitable sales into hard cash.

For those businesses that don't allow credit to their customers, the profits they generate from sales convert directly into cash surplus, no problem. However, for those that do allow credit there's a permanent time-lag between each sale and payment and if that lag gets too long, serious cash shortages can result.

Getting paid is a process – it's up to you to manage that process, no one else is going to do it for you.

Record how you do it

Written systems and procedures are indispensable for a growing business. This may seem like a sweeping statement when you consider this is a topic most small businesses completely ignore.

If you're really serious about saving yourself time, impressing your customers, making it easier to delegate and train your employees, building value and getting a real grip on how the whole business operates, you really can't overlook written systems. Systems for marketing activities, for instance, should be stitched in to all aspects of what you do and how you do it, thus allowing you to set the standards that pervade the whole business.

The advantages to be gained here are manifold and can make a huge positive difference both now and in the long-run.

People power

Your business is not an island. It cannot operate in isolation from the rest of the world – in some form or other you need the help and cooperation of others. No business can function or survive without willing customers and suppliers nor can it grow without the supportive labours of other people.

To harness this *people power* you need develop strong, long-lasting relationships with others – built on real trust, openness and a genuine will to do business for mutual benefit. This is the stuff of long-lasting working relationships!

By operating in this way you can not only harness the massive power of people who will go that extra mile to support your business, you'll also get the added satisfaction of knowing those people have truly benefited from dealing with you!

You really can do it

That bite-sized step in the development of your business is really important. It's not going to take you very long at all – perhaps just a few minutes – but when it's done you're that little bit closer to your goals.

Can you see the significance of this to you? It doesn't matter how busy your weekly work routines are, real tangible business development is accessible to you! *You really can do this*! Sure, your first few steps may be tentative and slow but once you get some forward motion all you need to do is keep it going... and going.

Stay patient and move forward with a steady pace you know you can maintain – start by reserving a bit of space in your diary each week: this will be *your time* for making a real difference to your business and your life!

The journey ahead

Imagine standing in the middle of foggy, bleak open moorland with no clue of which direction you need to go. What's more you're poorly equipped with no food or provisions and you don't even have a map or compass. Finding your way home might be a bit of challenge, right?

Of course, many of us would shudder at the thought of getting ourselves into such a difficult and dangerous position and yet, though they may not realise it, for most business start ups, this more or less describes the journey they're about to take. They usually set off without any real sense of where they are or want to go and, even where they do, they have little knowledge of what they'll need to do to get there.

The key aim of this book has been to clear some of that "fog" for you, to show you how to get clarity on where you want to be, to explain how to set out your path and to have greater control over the whole process that is... *kick-starting your business.*

If you've worked your way through all the preceding chapters you're now in a much stronger position to tackle the many challenges you'll face on your journey. What you've learned thus far has not provided you with the solution to every single challenge you'll meet but, at your fingertips, you now have a framework for dealing with most of them. What's more, you have the opportunity to avoid being a victim of what life throws at you and to take a strong and confident grip on your own destiny.

Being in business should be a constant learning experience: I hope that for you, this book marks the beginning of that process and I wish you well as you now embark upon the rest of your journey.

Further Reading

IF YOU wish to carry on strengthening and growing your business then you'll need to keep building your knowledge of what works and what doesn't work for you. There are many other popular writers out there with much to contribute to your ever-growing knowledge and you can easily find lists of great books on business-related websites. In particular you'll find a list of such books on Macrays site at **www.macrays.co.uk** in the business resources section.

I'd particularly like to share with you some titles that I feel are not only relevant to you as a small business owner but also capture those true underlying savvy ways of doing what you do...

Smart Perspective

In my research I've come across a number of writers who've focused much of their work on helping us to accept a way of thinking or a set of beliefs that help us to make decisions that support us in what we're trying to achieve. In this regard there are three particular books that stand out for me:

Million Dollar Consulting – **Alan Weiss**

As the name implies, this work is by a consultant primarily for consultants – but, if you're not in consultancy yourself, don't let this put you off! This guy is one very smart *hombre* and the underlying messages of this book, oozing with *savvy*, can be applied to any business. Weiss' remarks and observations cut straight to the heart of business issues we all face and will reward your time with a very different and powerful perspective.

The 7 Habits of Highly Effective People – **Steven Covey**

This widely recommended book is the product of many years of patient research and the result is a most insightful study of human nature and how we can harness that nature to make us more effective in our endeavours. I must confess I've read this book several times and regularly dip into it when I'm working with my clients.

True Professionalism – **David Maister**

Although this book was aimed at the so-called professional practice (lawyers, accountants, etc) it has huge value for any business.

This guy really tells it as it is and shows us that *True Professionalism* is more about attitude and the underlying quality of the way we work than about what profession we're in. If you're looking for excellence (and you should be because that's what your loyal customers seek) then this is a must read.

Getting your act together

Much has been said in this book about the importance of personal development; no doubt about it, business and personal growth go hand in hand. Many of your required new skills will relate directly to organising your business but inevitably there will be personal skills you'll need to work on. The three books referred to above, as well as covering a broad range of other aspects of business, will provide you with some invaluable insights.

There are two further books which, as a complement to these, will help you to better organise your daily routines and to stimulate your creative abilities:

Getting Things Done – David Allen

If you're looking for ways of organising your time with less stress, then this is a great resource. I can tell you that I've pulled techniques from this book that I now use in my day-to-day routines, saving me pots of time.

Mind Maps for Business – Tony Buzan and Chris Griffiths

There is a broad range of books on how to work with mind maps and what you can use them for. This work is the only one produced by Tony Buzan relating specifically to their applications for business. If this technique is of particular interest to you, you might also wish to take a look at software that makes it easier to generate and edit mind maps quickly and conveniently. You can find numerous suppliers through Google search.

Getting in touch with your customers

Any business owner with aspirations for growth will need to continually seek out new ways to better serve and communicate with their customers. Not surprisingly therefore there is a bewildering choice of books available, covering all aspects of the subject.

To begin with I'd suggest you focus on those books that take into account the time and financial limitations of the small business owner. As you develop and refine your approach you can start to look at more advanced stuff. Here are a couple of recommendations which will help you with those early tentative steps.

The Ultimate Small Business Marketing Book – Dee Blick

Dee Blick understands that small business owners don't have loads of time and are usually working on a fairly tight budget so you might wish to consider this highly popular book. The techniques you'll be introduced to here will give you a different perspective and help you take your marketing onto that next level... without breaking the bank. Highly recommended!

How to Get Clients to Come to You – **Nigel Temple**
This is a great, straight-to-the-point, introductory guide to the many marketing tools and techniques you can apply. Taking you through seven jargon-free steps for acquiring and retaining customers, this book will also provide you with a solid foundation for taking your next steps.

...and for the budding entrepreneur...

There are many books written by successful entrepreneurs who've *been there, done that,* most of whom can provide excellent practical guidance on how you can take your business onto another level. Here are three of my favourites to get you started:

The Richer Way – **Julian Richer**
You may have heard of the author's company Richer Sounds, which he set up from scratch and built into what subsequently became a well-known brand. The reader is given fascinating insights into the problems a fledgling business can face, the mistakes that can be made and how a successful business owner handles the challenges.

The Beermat Entrepreneur – **Mike Southon & Chris West**
This a nice gentle read, providing a fairly comprehensive guide to dealing with the challenges faced by businesses seeking substantial growth. If you're just starting out on a highly ambitious new project you'll find much of value here.

Losing My Virginity: The Autobiography – **Richard Branson**
This highly rated book provides interesting and important insights into how an entrepreneur thinks about, and makes, important business choices.

Testimonials

"It's so helpful to get advice about growing your business and where to go next."

Claire Drake
- Maldon Lettings

"As a young company we found Ian's genuine interest in small business both inspiring and motivating. After meetings we always come away feeling confident and energised. From the very beginning he was there to offer us step-by-step advice and that support has continued throughout the growth of our business. We have and will most definitely recommend him."

Jane and Penny Wyatt
– Directors - Penny Jane Flowers Limited

"Being part of a family run business can be challenging at times. In our meetings with Ian we had the opportunity to discuss our goals, assess the business performance, define job roles, find ways to become better managers. With Ian's guidance we left the meetings feeling energised. Moving forward Ian has helped us to put structure in place and run a better business."

Lorna Pissarro
– Director, Stuart Inns Limited

".... we have a greater feeling of confidence in the choices we make."

Derek Murton
– European Refrigeration Limited

"....impartial advice on what he thought we could improve on was invaluable advice. The meetings were packed with specific and relevant advice and it was great to draw on Ian's experience, which he has drawn from working with hundreds of businesses from all sectors of commerce."

Mark Williams
– Brainbox Candy Limited

"Ian has helped us make progress in really putting in place some business processes so we don't keep reinventing the wheel! Ian's style and method helps to really work on the business and make progress on our key objectives. With an easy to achieve process we have now made progress in some very important areas. He has made us think about our business and his sessions help us reflect on the issues moving forward. We always leave a session with actions and achieve our action plans enthusiastically after the meeting with Ian. Ian has also been extremely good at helping develop our brand. I would highly recommend working with Ian, businesses however small or large will benefit enormously. We started when there was just two of us in the business, we now have 41 and Ian's meetings are more and more relevant."

Andrew Macmillan
– Stuart Inns Ltd

"Macrays Accountants are very professional and I have pleasure in using their Business Adviser's service with great success."

Jason Lovell
– Wickford Diner

About the author

BORN IN South Yorkshire, Ian Marshall has worked in accountancy and managerial roles in London and the south-east of England for most of his career.

Having held senior roles in both large multinational companies and small business he has gradually built up a broad experience of the commercial world and a detailed understanding of what makes businesses tick.

Since 2001, he has specialised in helping small businesses to survive and grow through one-to-one consultancy, seminars and regular articles and newsletters. These resources have been aimed at providing savvy advice not otherwise readily available for small business owners and the particular challenges they face.

Ian is married to Ruth and they have two daughters.

Lightning Source UK Ltd.
Milton Keynes UK
UKOW06f1036190915

258891UK00002B/60/P